IS THERE
A GOD?

IS THERE A GOD?

QUESTIONS ABOUT SCIENCE AND THE BIBLE

IS THERE A GOD?

QUESTIONS ABOUT SCIENCE AND THE BIBLE

John M. Oakes, Ph.D.

Great Commission Illustrated
Long Beach, CA

WWW: http://greatcommission.com
Email: john_oakes@greatcommission.com

IS THERE A GOD?

QUESTIONS ABOUT SCIENCE AND THE BIBLE

Copyright © 1999 by John M. Oakes, Ph.D.

Published by Great Commission Illustrated

Printed in the United States of America

Second Printing, September, 1999

ISBN 0-9653469-9-4

Cover graphics and layout by William To

DEDICATION

To
Jan
Benjamin
Elizabeth and
Kathryn

ACKNOWLEDGMENTS

I would like to express my thanks, first of all to my wife, who never complained and always covered for me when I would slip out late at night or early in the morning to work on the book.

In addition, I would like to thank some people who have encouraged me in this project. These would include my good friends Gregg Marutzky and Gary Bishop who encouraged me a long time ago to use my training as a scientist to teach about evidences related to the Bible. In addition, Keith Tabor finally talked me into starting to write.

Thanks for help in the writing of this book goes to Douglas Jacoby who gave great encouragement and much needed criticism, as well as serving as a model of a Christian writer. Above all, I would like to thank my editor and publisher Rex Geissler whose dedication and skepticism have much to do with the final form of this book.

....the glory and greatness of Almighty God are marvelously discerned in all his works and divinely read in the open book of heaven.

Galileo Galilei

CONTENTS

FOREWORD

The need for biblical evidences is greater in our generation than ever before. Secularism and humanism are rampant, the media and the educational system bombard us with half-truths and untruths about the meaning of life, and multitudes are confused about the fundamentals of human existence. So profound is the confusion today that many ask not, "What are the answers?", but rather "What are the questions?" We in western society are in a bad way indeed! The need for fresh books—well thought out, well written, and well adapted to our generation—is phenomenal. I believe that, with this volume, you have acquired such a book.

For me it was fascinating to watch *Is There a God?* take shape, realizing what invaluable evidence John Oakes had brought to light. Christians the world over will appreciate its careful blend of science and Bible. My heart thrills at every piece of information, every perspective or new angle of entry to apologetic questions. During high school and university years my faith was strengthened enormously through reading apologetic works, and it was through our mutual interest in apologetics that John and I first came into contact. Over the years I have built up a small library around the subject of evidences. I personally am proud to add this latest work, *Is There a God: Questions about Science and the Bible*, to my collection.

Surely every disciple will want to follow the flow of John Oakes' reasoning and master the arguments, in order better to be equipped to convince others about God's reality and the truth of his Word.

It is rare to find a man of high caliber and academic integrity serving the Lord both as university professor and disciple of Christ. Thanks to that precious combination a superb new book has been authored, and to you I gladly commend both it and its author. For I have every confidence that in this book you will find something to strengthen your faith in God's existence, wisdom, and power.

Douglas Jacoby
Washington DC

*Whence is it that nature does
nothing in vain; and whence arises
all that order and beauty which we
see in the world?*

Isaac Newton

INTRODUCTION

A few years ago on an episode of the ABC show "Nightline," a debate was held between the late Carl Sagan and Jerry Falwell. Carl Sagan, then professor of astronomy at Cornell University, presumed to speak for all scientists as he propounded the view that the known laws of science can be used to explain the origin of both the universe we live in and of all life on earth. Jerry Falwell, then the president of the Moral Majority, presumed to speak for all "Bible-believing Christians" as he supported the view that the universe itself is only a few thousand years old, and that all scientific evidence supports this view. Who "won" the debate? Obviously Carl Sagan, being a scientist who has thought a lot about this issue, had a great advantage. He managed to win the debate and to once again make Christians look like intellectual fools. Unfortunately, debates are not always won by those on the side of truth, but rather are usually won by the more eloquent and well prepared. A more important question than who won this classic debate between the atheist and creationist, would be who was right? The answer is that neither was correct!

As a professor of chemistry and physics (my Ph.D. is in chemical physics), I have often had the opportunity to help students struggling with questions on the interface between science and religion—questions which relate to scientific truth and the Bible. Having at different times been both a minister and a professor, I am often asked whether there is a contradiction between faith in the Bible and my knowledge of science. I cannot agree with the well-known evolutionist Niles Eldredge who has said that we should "take the position that religion and science are two utterly different domains of human experience" and have "little in common."[1] If the Bible is true, or for that matter if any of the world religions were true, there would be profound implications in the realm of science. Simply brushing that aside would not change the facts.

But let us go back to the debate between Falwell and Sagan. Why were they both wrong? Because in the case of Carl Sagan and the school of atheists he represents, as well as in the case of Jerry Falwell and the creationists he represents, there is a fundamental flaw in their mode of thinking. They are simply not approaching the evidence as scientists are supposed to treat data. The first chapter of this book will discuss the pitfalls most atheists and "creationists" fall into as well as propose a more useful and open-minded approach to thinking about this important issue of the interface between science and religion. Should creationism be taught in our schools? Should the atheistic explanation of the origin of the universe and of life be the basis of the science curriculum? Should science instructors teach both views, and let the students decide for themselves? Or should we avoid the debate entirely? These questions can be ignored, but they will not go away. Christians, and especially Christians who are students, are sure to eventually come up against questions such as, "Do you really believe in Adam and Eve? Oh come on... get with it!" The believer might then be confronted with a statement such as: "Anyone with any intelligence at all knows that man evolved from apes. Do you mean to say you don't believe in evolution? And you want me to take your belief in the Bible seriously? Right!..."

The majority of Christians devote little or no energy to considering these questions. There are several reasons for this. First, they believe in the Bible by faith. No matter how hard it is for a non-believer to understand, many people believe the entire Bible is God-inspired. They take the flood account in Genesis, and the account of Adam and Eve at face value, just as much as they take the Bible's claim that Jesus Christ was a real person at face value. Whether or not an individual Christian has done enough research and study to verify for themselves this belief, inerrancy is clearly a claim of the Bible.[2] The fact that many followers of Jesus Christ accept the inerrancy of the Bible by faith is paradoxically one reason that they

---

[1] Niles Eldredge, *The Monkey Business* (Washington Square Press, New York, 1980), p. 10.

[2] See 2 Timothy 3:16 as an example of this claim in the Bible.

do not typically spend a lot of time concerned with testing the
scientific accuracy of the Bible. It is not hard to see how this could
create an intellectual inconsistency. One of the purposes of this book
is to address this problem.

Another reason followers of Jesus tend not to spend a lot of
mental energy considering these questions is that it simply is not an
issue of importance in their daily lives. There are hundreds of issues
which could be debated regarding Christianity and the Bible. When
will Jesus come back? What about the people who never heard about
Jesus? What about the "rapture"?

The list could go on seemingly indefinitely. Believers should ask
themselves: "Does this issue affect my or anyone else's eternal
destiny" or "Does this question affect how I will live my life today?"
If the answer to both questions is no, then one has found an issue
which is probably worth little if any time debating. In the words of
Galileo: "Can an opinion be heretical, and yet have no concern with
the salvation of souls?" [3] It would not seem, at least at first glance,
that one's view of the creation story in Genesis is relevant to
salvation or to how one should live their life in a practical way on an
every day basis. However, a case will be made in this chapter that
these issues are nevertheless important enough for all believers to
spend time thinking about.

A third reason most Christians do not spend a lot of time
focusing on this issue is that most of them are not scientists. Even if a
follower of Jesus wanted to consider these questions in an intelligent
way, they probably would not even know where to begin. For this
reason, it is easy to fall into the trap of just ignoring the issue or
perhaps reading one book which agrees with one's own pre-
conceived opinion, and not seriously questioning the arguments put
forth in the book. Granted, one's interpretation of the first chapter of
Genesis may not be a salvation issue or even a practical matter
effecting how a person lives his life this week. Granted, most
Christians are still a bit short of their Ph.D. in physics. Nevertheless,
there are many reasons ignoring questions relating to science and the
Bible would be a mistake. Some of those reasons will be listed in
this introduction. Questions about science and the Bible will
inevitably come up at one time or another. Why not face them now?

One reason disciples of Jesus need to face these questions is

---

[3] Galileo Galilei, excerpted from a letter to the Grand Duchess Christina, 1614.

illustrated by the passage of 1 Peter 3:15-16.

> Always be prepared to give an answer to everyone who asks you to give the reason for the hope you have. But do this with gentleness and respect, keeping a clear conscience, so that those who speak maliciously against your good behavior in Christ may be ashamed of their slander.

If a sincere question is asked of a believer such as "what does the Bible teach about evolution?" and a flippant response is given, such as, "where is your faith?" that would clearly not square with this command in the Bible. If a person is ignorant on the subject, the best answer is a simple, "I don't know," not a manipulative attempt to deflect the question. Furthermore, according to the scripture just quoted, a Christian has a responsibility to "be prepared to give an answer." This book is an attempt to help readers move toward that goal.

Many believers have often heard questions such as, "what about evolution and the Bible?" At times, questions like these can be a smoke screen on the part of a person who is not yet ready face up to the issues God is raising in his or her life. An example of this sort of interaction is recorded in John 4:7-26. When Jesus confronted a woman about the sin in her life, she immediately changed the subject to a religious issue without the personal implications of dealing with her own sin. Jesus answered her question with gentleness and respect, which ultimately led to her conversion. Unfortunately, this is not always the result, as some would rather debate abstract ideas than deal with the need for repentance in their lives. While some people raise questions of science and religion out of a desire simply to argue, it is also true that questions relating to science and the Bible sometimes come from people who are sincerely seeking the truth. Those who believe in the Bible must prepare themselves to give a carefully reasoned argument in answer to these questions.

A second reason followers of Jesus need to be prepared to answer these questions relates to their children. It is a fact that as a matter of public policy as well as of general consensus, the atheistic approach to interpreting knowledge about science is presented to kids from grade school through graduate school. Parents cannot afford to sit back and say "Que será, será." The faith of their children is at issue. Students will tend to accept what they are taught at face value.

Parents must be prepared to discuss with their children the truth
about the creation of the universe and of life. Where will they get it if
not from home? A simplistic explanation from parents or church
leaders which is not even consistent with the known facts of science
is insufficient.

Children ask a lot of questions in their early years. They are
smart enough to see through a shallow explanation without a sound
basis. Perhaps one day you will take a family trip to the Grand
Canyon and it will finally hit your child that the explanations they are
reading in the park brochures are in apparent agreement with what
they are seeing in front of their eyes, but in apparent dramatic
contrast with what they have heard from you or someone else they
respect in a church setting. The children will ask those hard
questions; guaranteed. What will be said in response? The quality of
the answer may have a dramatic effect on the child who hears it. To
the extent it is possible, children must be presented the truth, not a
cover-up.

A third reason one must be prepared to answer the questions
raised in this book is for the sake of their own faith. Surely by now
you have asked them yourself how what is recorded in Genesis 1
relates to what was learned in science classes. The lazy mind tends to
put unanswered questions under the rug. The problem is that things
shoved under the rug can come back to bite. Perhaps at some point in
a believer's life things will be going great, but at his point of greatest
weakness or discouragement, Satan will attack. Nagging doubts about
the inspiration of the Bible are a potential Achilles' heel a Christian
cannot afford to ignore.

Jesus himself learned this lesson as described in Luke 4:1-12,
when Satan attacked him at the end of a forty-day fast. Satan's attack,
in part, was an attempt to get Jesus to question the authority of God's
word. The wrong time to build defenses is while the battle is raging.
It may be a gradual process, but nagging doubts eventually need to be
nailed down with the truth!

There are many books written on the general subject of the
relationship of science and religion, and in particular on the
relationship between science and the Bible. Nevertheless, in having
read a good number of them, I have always found myself feeling that
there was a great deal missing from these books about science and the
Bible. These works typically fall into two categories. They tend to
either have very poor science, or they seem to be attempts to

apologize for and to explain away the Bible. Eventually, I felt compelled to fill the void and write a book which dealt with science in an honest and forthright way without trying to explain away the Bible.

There are three thoughts I have tried to keep in mind in writing this book. First, I have assumed the reader is relatively unfamiliar with the scientific issues involved, and have therefore filled in at least a sketch of the widely held views of most scientists in the areas touched on in the book. Second, I have attempted to avoid the sarcastic tone I feel many authors writing in this area tend to slip into. Third, I have taken pains to only present scientific conclusions, which I believe are supported by the preponderance of the scientific evidence. This would contrast with many theories of the creationist and atheist camps, which fit neatly with their respective beliefs about science and religion, yet are at best possibilities with scant "science" to back them up.

It is impossible for anyone to be an expert in all the areas of science dealt with in this book. I have attempted to emphasize those in which I have significant expertise, and to some extent focus less on those in which I have only a shallow background. I apologize in advance for any errors which I may have made in fields such as geology and evolution where my background is relatively weak.

John M. Oakes
Fond du Lac, Wisconsin, January, 1999

*What can be accounted for by fewer
assumptions is explained in vain by
more.*

William of Ockham

1

HOW SHOULD I THINK?

One may ask, "are you trying to tell me how to think?" Well, yes, in a way. This book contains a suggested way of thinking to approach scientific evidence which will dramatically improve the probability of arriving at the truth. It just so happens that this approach will work in most any investigation, not just in scientific questions. Stated quite simply, when asking a question about the truth, let the facts determine the answer. Possibly the biggest impediment to a person finding the truth when examining a question is assuming the answer to the question before even starting the investigation. Someone might answer, "Surely, I would never do that! I am totally open-minded." It might be helpful for that person to consider that it is human nature to be closed minded about certain things.

In my many hours of counseling people with a great range of problems in their lives, I have found that one fact comes out again and again. If our sense of security, sense of being loved, sense of well-being, pride, or simple desire to pursue pleasure are at risk, we will readily believe in almost any lie, whether it is told by others or from our own invention, if it is consistent with what makes us feel more comfortable.

An alcoholic is a victim. Premarital sex is a good idea to determine if two people are compatible. I could never get AIDS. People can take advantage of each other and still be great friends. A woman can change an abusive guy by staying with him. It is OK for a taxpayer to cheat on his taxes, after all, everyone else does it. If someone is feeling bad, overeating will make it go away. Success in a career will make a person happy. Lies, Lies, Lies!!

Every one of these statements is a lie! At one level or another, we know they are all lies. Yet, at one time or another all of us have believed some of these lies. Why? It is difficult for us to accept the truth. The truth can be threatening intellectually or emotionally or in some other way. Nevertheless, we would do ourselves a favor to admit that our human nature makes us prone to believe lies if we do not closely watch ourselves. We don't want people "telling us" the truth.

Are scientists human? That is an easy one. Contrary to a commonly held myth, scientists are subject to the same weaknesses as the rest of humanity. Scientists have not exactly tried to dispel the public perception that they are somehow almost infallible. It is a common joke of our society that doctors try to create the impression of infallibility. Scientists tend to fall into the same trap. A closer look at the history of science will reveal this truth. Scientists as a group have always been highly resistant to changing their long-held beliefs. In general, scientists are aware of this tendency, but seem to succumb to the pitfall anyway. Why? Scientists are people. Despite this (or perhaps because of this tendency), we should bear in mind the words of Thoreau, "No way of thinking, no matter how ancient, should be accepted without proof."[1]

There are many famous examples of scientists who had the nerve to propose a new theory (which just happened to be correct) only to be initially rejected by the scientific establishment unprepared to have their boat rocked. In some cases, scientists were even initially persecuted for propounding theories which are now universally accepted. For example, consider the story of the German scientist Jacobus van't Hoff. Organic chemists of his day had a belief that when a carbon atom had four atoms bonded to it, the resulting molecule had a flat shape with the four attached atoms at right angles to one another. While still a graduate student in 1874, van't Hoff proposed that carbon actually had a three-dimensional, tetrahedral shape (like a three-sided pyramid with carbon at the center of the pyramid) when it carried four substituent atoms. Not surprisingly, other notable scientists of his day did not easily accept this new view,

---

[1] From *Walden* by Henry David Thoreau.

despite the fact that it readily explained some known facts which were inconsistent with the currently held theory. He was actually persecuted, being temporarily blacklisted and unable to obtain a position as a chemistry professor. Eventually, the old guard was forced to give in as the huge weight of evidence supported the tetrahedral theory.

This story is by no means an isolated example. In fact, for large shifts in scientific models, it has been the rule rather than the exception. A certain amount of skepticism to new and untried ideas is not only appropriate but also necessary for scientists in their work. However, the scientific method absolutely requires an open mind in order to function.

Why were the scientists of van't Hoff's day so closed-minded? For the same reasons that people in general are. Their pride was at stake, for one thing. Also, it is always easier to continue thinking the way one was trained to think. This is no less true for scientists than for others. They might have even had to change their lecture notes. Imagine that!

As another example, when Isaac Newton first proposed the Law of gravity, Gottfried Leibniz (Newton's co-inventor of calculus) vilified him. Leibniz accused Newton of heresy, because his belief in the attraction of objects to one another by "gravity" was "subversive of natural, and inferential revealed religion." In other words, Leibniz was claiming that the theory of gravity not only contradicted the evidence—it also contradicted the Bible. One could assume that if Leibniz were alive today, he would not make this statement. Did the theory of gravity disagree with the data or the Bible? No! It disagreed with the commonly held view of its day.

PRE-CONCEIVED NOTIONS

These examples have a direct relation to the debate which has raged between atheists and creationists. It would be helpful to first give a careful definition of both the atheists' and the creationists' view of the natural world. The atheists' view of nature can be explained as follows:

EVERY EVENT WHICH HAS EVER OCCURRED OR EVER WILL OCCUR IN THE UNIVERSE CAN BE EXPLAINED BY THE LAWS OF NATURE.

For the atheist, supernatural explanations are summarily rejected out of hand. According to this view, the scientist's job, then, is to discover these laws of nature, and use them to explain such difficult questions as the origin of the universe, the origin of life, the origin of species, and the geology and structure of the earth as it now exists. A quote from John Desmond Bernal in his book *The Origins of Life* serves to represent this view.

> Now with both of these alternatives—self-ordering or transcendent design—it is always open to the skeptic to refuse to choose between them. However, in practice, the skeptic can only concentrate on the materialist alternative because this is the only one which gives anything to argue about or experiment with. [2]

In other words, in choosing to look at the evidence nature offers to us, a scientist can choose to consider possible transcendent explanations (for example the possibility that God may exist), or one can assume that these things must be explained by the laws of nature. Scientists such as Bernal, and atheists in general, choose up front to assume the origin of the universe, of life, and so forth all have a natural explanation. They do not even allow for the possibility of a miraculous explanation. This, the standard position of atheists, is clearly an example of a pre-conceived notion. Bernal is more honest about his way of thinking than most other atheists are! Let it be said again. The basic assumption made by many, if not most scientists, that there are not now, nor have there ever been supernatural events is just that, an assumption. The conclusions of these people can be no better than their assumptions.

As an example of application of this principle to a specific issue—the origin of man, a quote from Thomas Huxley, the nineteenth century biologist (and grandfather of Aldous Huxley, the author of the book *Brave New World*) would be appropriate. In referring to how man came to be he says:

> We are as much a product of blind forces as is the falling of a stone to earth, or the ebb and flow of the tides.

---

[2] John Desmond Bernal, *The Origin of Life,* (Weidendorf and Nicolson, London,1967), p. 140.

We have just happened, and man was made flesh by a long series of singularly beneficial accidents.

It will be shown that this amounts to a religious statement of faith, and that belief in this precept requires a much greater leap of faith than belief in the God of the Bible.

CREATIONISM

What is creationism? Creation scientists may not fit as easily into a box, but the perspective on the natural world of many creationists may be summed up in a fairly simple statement as follows:

THE UNIVERSE IS A FEW THOUSAND YEARS OLD. THE PREPONDERANCE OF KNOWN SCIENTIFIC FACTS ARE IN AGREEMENT WITH THIS CLAIM.

Many creationists feel that all faithful Christians should agree with this statement, and that their theory should be taught on at least an equal footing with the atheistic view in public schools. This has led to considerable controversy across the United States. As a statement which could represent the typical view of creationists, consider a quote from the book *Scientific Creationism* by Henry Morris, a leader in the creationist movement.

In the preceding chapters it has been shown that the basic facts of science today fit the special creation model much better than they do the evolution model. Although there are certain problems that still need solutions, none are of sufficient gravity to disturb the basic creation framework, whereas the many problems in the evolution model are serious.[3]

By the phrase the "special creation model," the author means the view that the earth was created no earlier than "about 5500 BC at most," quoting the same author. Morris in his book does point out some interesting problems of the evolutionary theory, but the claim

---

[3] Henry M. Morris, *Scientific Creationism* (Master Books, El Cajon, California, 1974), p. 203.

that the weight of evidence supports the idea that the earth is only a few thousand years old is not supported by the evidence. This point will be discussed in some detail in the second chapter.[4]

It would be fair to point out that not all scientists who would call themselves creationists would agree with the viewpoint described above. Some would call themselves "old earth creationists." These scientists take the view that the universe and all forms of life were created by God, but would contend that the evidence supports the existence of the universe and of life for a vastly greater span of time. This view is described and to some extent defended in this book. However, to keep it simple (with apologies to the "old earth creationists"), in this book, the term creationist will be used to describe those who would hold to the young earth viewpoint.[5]

A central tenet of this book is that the claims of both atheists and creationists do not stand up to even a simple scientific scrutiny, but that the Bible, if understood correctly, does agree with what we know from science. In other words, the debate between the atheists and the creationists is one between two groups, both of whose assumptions and conclusions are way off the mark.

Both the atheists and the creationists go wrong because their approach to truth has a deep and fundamental flaw. They assume the answer to their question before they even begin to ask it. A study both of history and of everyday human experience will show convincingly that if a person or group of people make a firm choice to believe something, they will be able to bend, edit, alter, misinterpret or even lie about the evidence until they have "proved" their point. It will be shown in chapters three and four that atheists

---

[4] As an example of the tendency toward preconceived notions, consider also the comment from Frank Lewis Marsh (a seventh day Adventist, Ph.D. biologist, and well know member of the creationist-oriented Geoscience Research Institute): "In my opinion, we cannot use our senses in the manner of uniformitarians in interpreting what we see in the earth....This is an extremely important point. Special Revelation takes precedence over natural revelation because natural science can be correct only when in harmony with special Revelation." This is a excerpt from a letter of 1962 to George McCready Price, a leader in the flood geology movement, from the Marsh Papers. In other words, if scientific evidence and the Bible appear to disagree, we will assume the Bible is right, and basically ignore the scientific evidence.

[5] A very thorough and surprisingly fair-minded treatment of the various strains of the modern creationist movement is found in the reference; Ronald L. Numbers, *The Creationist: The Evolution of Scientific Creationism* (University of California Press, Berkeley, California, 1992). Note: this reference book is not for the faint hearted reader!

are forced to play these same intellectual games in order to conclude what they already believe by faith, namely that God does not exist.

A well-known example of a group of people who reached a "scientific" conclusion due to their pre-conceived opinion would be that of the so-called scientific research done under the Nazi regime to prove that the Germans/Aryans were the superior race of humanity. Hitler had MDs and Ph.D.s, such as Ley and Goebels, lined up behind him with plenty of scientific facts to back up their perverted theories. It seems doubtful that there were any blacks, Latinos, or Asians on the committee to reach this unbiased, scientific conclusion. It would certainly not be fair to compare creationists or atheists in general to the Nazi regime. In fact, the great majority of both creationists and atheists are quite sincere in their intentions. However, this serves to illustrate the danger of having an emotional or political agenda motivating scientific research.

Speaking of making the mistake of assuming the answer before one asks the question, what about professed Christians? Do they make the same mistake? The answer is absolutely yes. Unfortunately, many believers have a lazy mindset, not wanting to ask those hard questions. If, in studying the Bible, one assumes it is true without even questioning whether it agrees with what is known to be true about the world, then how deep is their faith? Why should a person believe the Word of God is inspired (2 Timothy 3:16)? Why should they believe Jesus Christ was raised from the dead? In Acts 17:10-12, the Berean people were commended by God both for their open-minded enthusiasm and for having enough healthy skepticism to check out in the Bible if what Paul said was true. If the Bible is truly from God, then it will stand up to any level of honest and sincere criticism. For example, someone believes in the Bible. Maybe they were just lucky. Maybe if the same person had been exposed to the Qur'an (the scripture of Islam) first, they would be a Muslim today.

If, in asking questions about the Bible and science, one is unwilling to reach the conclusion that the Bible is wrong, then it is easy to predict what conclusion will be reached. But what good is a conclusion reached using the same approach that the atheists use? Faith in the truth is something which needs to be deepened. This cannot happen unless believers are willing to look at the world around them and deal with the truth. Those who would claim to follow Jesus Christ need to set an example for the world in right thinking, not just right living.

There are plenty of examples from history of religious people claiming to have the authority of scripture to back up their opinions and using this inferred authority to suppress the truth about the laws of nature. As one example, consider the Roman Curia as it accused Galileo of heresy for teaching that the earth travels around the sun, rather than the sun around the earth. To quote the Catholic curia, "an opinion can in no wise be probable which has been declared and defined to be contrary to Divine Scripture."[6]

In other words, "no matter how much evidence exists to the contrary, you need to believe our own narrow, private interpretation of the Bible." A more reasonable view would be that if something is obviously not true, people should stop believing it. If the Bible is the inspired creation of God, then its truth should hold up to careful inspection. To quote Galileo's defense of the Copernican theory of the sun-centered solar system:

> ...to bar Copernicus now, would seem in my judgement, to be a contravention of truth, and an attempt to hide and suppress her the more as she revealed herself more clearly and plainly.[7]

FAITH OR FACT?

Another common error in thinking that many professed Christians make is to confuse what they know by faith with what they know by fact. A few personal examples will make the point. I know by fact, from a careful investigation on my own over years of careful study, that Jesus Christ was resurrected from the dead (supporting this claim would require another book). On the other hand, I believe by faith that heaven exists. There is no concrete evidence to support the idea that heaven exists. In fact, according to the Bible, heaven is a thing of the future, not the present. Nevertheless, I believe in heaven because the Bible, a book I am convinced is inspired, talks about it.

Because of a careful study of historical evidence, I believe by fact that the Bible is an accurate historical document. Being an amateur historian, I have taken the time to check it out, hopefully in an open-minded way by reading numerous books, some written by non-believers. For example, it can be shown from archaeological

---

[6] An excerpt from the Roman Curia's sentence statement to Galileo, 1632.

[7] An excerpt from Galileo's letter to the Grand Duchess Christina, 1614.

evidence that King David is an actual historical figure. Similarly, the account in the Bible of Judah being conquered by Nebuchudnezzar is confirmed by historical and archaeological evidence. The city of Nineveh is real, not just part of a Biblical fantasy as some in the nineteenth century claimed. Skeptics in the past have called all these Biblical claims into question, but now archaeological evidence supports these accounts. On the other hand, I believe that Jesus will "come again to judge the living and the dead" because it says so in the Bible. There exists a mountain of reasons, including some described in this book to believe the Bible is the inspired Word of God. Therefore I believe its claim that Jesus will come again. There is no direct evidence to present to support the belief that Jesus will come again. No one can go out and dig up proof. It can only be believed by faith.

If a skeptic has a hard time believing Jesus will come back to the earth, it would be hard to blame him. A careful inspection of the world around us would certainly not lead one to believe that Jesus will come back to the earth as described in the Bible. However, one could point this person to the Bible and the mass of evidence supporting its inspiration, and admit they believe it by faith. It is a mistake to forget to separate what is believed because of the evidence from what is believed because of faith in the authority of the Bible.

As another example of identifying whether something is believed by fact or by faith, I believe Adam and Eve existed. Why? Because it is stated to be true in the Bible. Is there any direct evidence to support this claim, any historical or archaeological data? No. No one has yet discovered a radiocarbon-dated cave inscription such as, "Adam and Eve slept here." It would be a mistake to deceive oneself or anyone else on this point. Belief in the existence of the actual persons Adam and Eve can only be by faith.

Although there is no physical evidence to offer that Adam and Eve existed, the Bible account is not in direct conflict with any known fact of science. Yes, it is true that the evidence from paleontology shows that Australopithecine lived before man. Yes, it is true that apes and men have a virtually identical genetic code. Nevertheless, if the Bible is inspired by God, then two conclusions seem inescapable. First, Adam and Eve were created and second, their creation was a supernatural event. Supernatural events, if they do occur, by their very nature do not lend themselves well to scientific investigation. However the overwhelming evidence to support belief in the inspiration of the Bible could cause a person to believe this supernatural event occurred. The subject of creation versus evolution of man is discussed in chapter nine.

For the sake of clarity, the term miracle should be defined. A miracle is by definition an event that defies the laws of nature. It is a "supernatural event." Some of the miracles described in the Bible can only be believed by faith in the power of God and the truthfulness of the writer. Other miracles described in the Bible can be believed because of the evidence. One of the strongest claims of this book— one which will be proven beyond a reasonable doubt, is that life was created. The first living thing was produced by an act of creation. If true, then that was surely a supernatural event! Here, then, is a miracle described by the Bible, which can be believed because of the evidence.

The mistake of not being willing to separate faith from fact is a major factor in the errors of the creationists. If God created the world, whether in six days or fifteen billion years, it is still a supernatural event, without scientific "explanation." So why bend the data to agree with your own private interpretation about how God did it? If God created the earth with an appearance of age, then it will appear old. Why try to claim it appears young, when even the simplest look at the evidence known to students at the junior high school level would tell you that the world appears to be at the very least many millions of years old? The age of the earth will be considered in some detail in the next chapter.

FOR TODAY

1. Can you think of any "theories" you have held on to in the past which you later had to give up in light of new evidence or information? What did that feel like?

2. Do you agree with the creationist's view of nature as described in this chapter?

3. Do you agree with the atheist's view as described in this chapter?

4. If the answer to the two previous questions is no, what do you believe, or are you simply not sure?

5. Can you identify any "pre-conceived notions" you bring into reading this book that relate to science and religion?

6. Where do you believe the concept of "healthy skepticism" fits in with faith?

7. Can you think of something you believe in "by faith" as opposed to something you believe in because of the evidence?

8. Are there any nagging questions relating to science and the Bible which you have left unanswered? What are they? (It is a good habit to write questions like these down to be dealt with at a later time.)

True assumptions must save the
appearances.

Nikolai Copernicus

2

How Old is the Earth?

How old is the earth? That is a good question. Although I could provide my best estimate based on the scientific evidence, I can honestly say I do not know. One thing which can be said with confidence (as will be shown in this chapter) is that the earth *appears* to be very old. How old? Well, that depends on what evidence you choose to look at; uranium dating, the core temperature of the earth, the amount of salt in the oceans or any of a number of other more or less valid measures.

Actually there are two separate but related questions which could be asked. How old is the earth, and how old is the universe itself? In considering evidence related to the age of the universe, one could ask about the distance to the farthest known celestial objects, or consider the theories of the origin and life cycle of stars and galaxies. In the end, upon looking at all the evidence, whether one concludes that the earth appears to be one hundred million years old or ten billion years old does not seem to matter. If in fact the earth appears to be extremely old, then the assumption of special creation as defined by the creationists is in big trouble, because an age of seven thousand years or even ten thousand years is out of this range, to say the least.

One other possibility to consider is that the earth was created "with an appearance of age." In other words, one ought to consider the possibility that the universe was created in a well-evolved state so that it already appeared to be extremely old at the first instant of creation. This intriguing possibility will complicate the discussion of the scientific facts, but in an open-minded search for the truth about origins it must be considered. This possibility will be discussed in due time, but at this point it might be helpful to ask oneself what the possible implications would be for what would likely be observed in nature if it were true that the earth was created "with an appearance of age."

Does it really matter how old the earth is? It would be fair to admit that it is not a factor most people take into account in choosing their career, or their friends, or for that matter what brand of toothpaste to buy. Nevertheless, as stated in the introduction, there are several reasons to spend some time considering these issues. How does the claim that the earth appears to be very old make you feel as a Christian? Does it challenge some long-held beliefs? Some people are even made angry when they hear this claim. The reader's job is to take what he already knows by both fact and faith and to be willing to take an honest, open-minded look at this question.

There exist a very great number of facts discovered by scientists which support the view that the earth and the universe are very old. In this chapter just a few examples will be given which will show that the earth appears to be very old, certainly at least many millions of years old.

DISTANCE OF CELESTIAL OBJECTS

Consider, for example, the distance of celestial objects. For relatively close (by cosmological standards) objects, scientists use the method of parallax viewing of stars and galaxies to determine the distance to these objects in the sky. Basically, this method amounts to looking at both a relatively nearer and a relatively farther object in the sky from two distant points, say from where the earth is in the spring and where the earth is in the fall. The nearer object will appear to move just slightly with respect to the farther object. The angle of displacement determines the distance to the farther object or the nearer object, whichever was not previously known.

Using Parallax to determine the distance of a star.

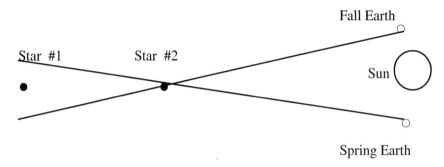

Figure 2.1
In the fall, star #2 appears to be to the right of star #1, while in the spring, star #2 appears to be to the left of star #1.

Another method used to estimate the distance to extremely distant objects such as quasars involves looking at the size of the "red shift" of light from those objects. The red shift will be discussed in some detail in a later chapter. There are other methods of estimating the distance to extremely remote objects such as looking at the relative brightness and size of very distant galaxies and estimating their distance by assuming the absolute size of the galaxies are at least similar to that of ones closer to us. Even if the skeptic chose to dismiss some of these distance-measuring techniques, they would be faced with the inescapable fact that there are billions of galaxies in the universe, each containing billions of stars. The known universe is clearly very, very big!

Use as an example the spiral galaxy M31 in Andromeda. It is 2.25 million light years from our solar system. How long ago did the light hitting an astronomer's telescope leave this galaxy? Since light travels a distance of one light year per year (that is the definition of a light year), evidently the galaxy being viewed is at least 2.25 million years old (actually, using the evolutionary theory of stars, cosmologists would predict many of the stars in the Andromeda galaxy to be billions of years old) because the light being viewed today left that galaxy 2.25 million years ago. In fact, looking at extremely distant objects is one way scientists can literally look into the past. The most distant known objects are quasars, which appear to be billions of light years from us. Presumably, when one observes these quasars, they are viewing light which was emitted from the objects billions of years ago. The conclusion from this evidence is that the universe *appears* to be at least a few billion years old.

Does this evidence prove absolutely that the universe is billions of years old? The answer is no, it does not. An all-knowing, all-powerful God such as the one described in the Bible could certainly create stars out of nothing. In fact, logically, if a star was created seven thousand years ago at a distance seven thousand and one light years from us, it should suddenly pop into view some time in the next year. We do not see stars suddenly popping into view, so we naturally conclude that an object such as the spiral galaxy M31 is at least 2.25 million years old. However, a God who could create a galaxy out of nothing could also simultaneously create light to be in transit from that distant galaxy to here at the point of creation, making it appear that the star is millions of years old, rather than only several thousand years. This argument may not sound convincing, but the fact is that we are not in a position to ultimately "prove" the age of an extremely distant object. The point is this: by this scientific evidence the universe appears old. The actual age is another question, but the universe certainly appears very much older than seven thousand years using this evidence. Please let us not claim otherwise.

How do the creationists deal with this question? Creationists have attempted to deal with the evidence by calling into question the use of Euclidean geometry.[1] Einstein's theory of special relativity implies that space is curved, requiring the use of what is called Riemannian geometry to describe space. This is all well and good. However, whether one uses Euclidean geometry, or Riemannian, it would probably be safe to say that there is not a physicist alive today (except perhaps a young earth creationist) who would agree that Riemannian geometry could support the idea that light could travel ten billion light years in just a few thousand years.

Another creationist attempt to defend the young earth view in light of the apparent size of the universe is to claim that the speed of light has changed over time.[2] This is a remarkable claim! The constant value of the speed of light is the underpinning assumption of

[1] For example, H. S. Slusher, *Age of the Cosmos* (Institute for Creation Research, San Diego, California, 1980), pp. 33-37.
[2] For example, Walt Brown, *In the Beginning* (Center for Scientific Creation, Phoenix, Arizona, 1995), pp. 158-161.

the theory of relativity. Let it be put simply—there is no credible support to the claim that the speed of light has changed over time. A thorough treatment of this claim can be found in a book by Alan Hayward.[3] Let us just admit it, the universe appears old. Whether it is one hundred million or one hundred billion is beside the point. The universe appears to be very old.

GEOLOGICAL DEPOSITS

Another piece of evidence for the earth itself being old is the clearly defined layers in the sedimentary deposits on the earth. Geologists call these alluvial deposits. As an example, anyone who has ever been to the Grand Canyon will immediately notice that there are many thousands of nearly horizontal layers of rock with a total thickness of about six thousand feet. These are sedimentary rocks, which reason would seem to imply must have been laid down over great periods of time by deposits of sand, dirt, dust and organic matter. In fact, the column of sedimentary rock on the earth's surface is as much as sixteen miles (80,000 ft) deep in places. It averages over one mile in depth over the entire land surface of the earth.

How did these thousands, and in some cases many millions of layers of rock get there? Is there any analogy to the rings one can find in trees? The answer is yes. For example, consider the Green River shale deposits in Colorado and Utah. Here up to several million pairs of alternating light and dark layers of sediment can be found right on top of one another. By looking for fossilized pollen remnants, it can be shown that the dark layers represent the spring and summer seasons, while lighter, pollen-free layers represent sediment laid down in the fall and winter. Here we see what seems to be clear evidence that this area was for at least several million years a region of fairly shallow "inland sea."

Consider as well the Bahama banks—the geological formation on top of which sits the islands of the Bahamas, off the coast of Florida. Drilling into the surface has shown that underlying the Bahamas area is a deposit of almost pure limestone approximately 18,000 feet deep. The most reasonable conclusion is that this limestone deposit was laid down over a great period of time by the coral reefs. The process of growth is still visible today. The rate at

---

[3] Alan Hayward, *Creation and Evolution* (Bethany House Publishers, Minneapolis, Minnesota, 1995), pp. 99-102.

Figure 2.2 Sedimentary rock showing strata or layers in the Grand Canyon.

which limestone is created by the coral and other creatures living in a reef can be debated (it has been estimated[4] at about one inch in one hundred years). Besides, it can be assumed that the rate would not be constant, as variations in climate would certainly affect the rate of growth of the deposits. Nevertheless, one is left with clear and seemingly incontrovertible evidence that the reefs have existed for many millions of years.

Returning to the Grand Canyon, one could attempt to actually count the layers or to quote a depth-per-year estimate in an attempt to estimate the age of the lowest layers at the canyon. Whether the sediments were deposited at an average rate of one millimeter per year or one inch per year, the numbers calculated for the age of the lowest layers would be many millions of years.

The fact is that creationists claim that the layers at the Grand Canyon, all six thousand feet of them, were laid down in the seven thousand years or so the earth has been around. Not only that, but they would claim the millions of pairs of layers in the Green River shale formation, the Bahama Banks and indeed all the sedimentary layers over the entire earth were all laid down within the few

---

[4] D. E. Wonderly, *Time-Records in Ancient Sediments*, (Crystal Press, 1977), pp. 113-126.

thousand year history of the earth. On the surface, this claim seems to be simply not credible.

How do the creationists explain the sedimentary layers—up to eighty thousand feet deep in places? They claim that most or all of these layers were laid down in one great flood—the flood recorded in Genesis chapter six through nine. To quote from a book by Henry Morris, possibly the number one leader in the creationist movement:

> The question is simply whether the model of a single global cataclysm, primarily hydraulic in nature, can explain the data of geology better than the uniformitarian/multiple local catastrophe model.[5]

By "single global cataclysm, primarily hydraulic in nature," the author means the Noahic flood recorded in Genesis. This is a humorous way to refer to the flood. These authors claim that a single flood is the most reasonable explanation for up to 80,000 feet of sedimentary rock at the surface of the earth. One should ask at this point, is this a reasonable explanation? Sediment does not normally form into rock in this short a time.[6] Besides, a single flood could only distribute an amount of sediment equal to the soil and other loose material already at the surface of the earth when the flood occurred. In addition, the multitude of layers have unique chemical as well as fossil makeup, inconsistent with the one-flood idea.

Can anyone believe this explanation? The answer is yes, someone who has already made up his or her mind to reach this conclusion before even beginning to look at the evidence. The creationists have to perform great feats of contortion to explain how the older fossils always seem to be below the younger fossils. For example, trilobites, when found with dinosaurs are always below them, while the great mammals are always above the dinosaurs, except in the rare exceptions of overthrust faults. Creationists believe all these species lived at the same time and somehow during the flood

---

[5] Henry M. Morris and Gary E. Parker, *What is Creation Science?*, (Master Books, El Cajon, California, 1987), p. 248.

[6] Special cases have been noted in which sediments can form into rocks fairly quickly. For example, under exceptional circumstances, limestone known as "beachrock" can form on tropical beaches within just a few years. Nevertheless, for the more typical examples such as shale formed from mud or sandstone, the sedimentary rocks mentioned in this section form only after very long time and usually under great pressure.

the trilobites got sorted out from the dinosaurs, which got sorted out from the mammals and so forth by various sorting mechanisms.[7]

Despite the fact that the creationist attempt to explain the fossil record and the alluvial layers falls apart of its own weight, they hope that if they can introduce one piece of evidence which might legitimately call into question the theory that the earth is very old they may cause people to accept the idea that their theory deserves equal time.

Perhaps the most famous example of an attempt of this type was in the supposed discovery of human and dinosaur footprints in the same rock formation. The most well known and publicized example is known as the Paluxy man tracks, found near Glen Rose, Texas. Films such as *Footprints in Stone* have been produced which purport to show "scientifically" that dinosaurs and people lived at the same time. If this claim were true, it would certainly turn the current system of chronology used by paleontologists on its tail.

Upon careful study of the actual evidence,[8] the dinosaur footprints appear to be genuine, but the "human" prints have been shown to be either random deformations in the rock, misinterpreted dinosaur prints, or recent carvings. Even some of the original creationist investigators have since backed down on their claims that these tracks are legitimate evidence to support the claim that dinosaurs and people once lived together. Interestingly, young-earth believers have at times referred to this claim as proven.[9] The problem is that once word gets out that there is scientific "proof" that man and dinosaurs lived at the same time, it is hard to "put the genie back in the bottle." It can be predicted that for many years to come, sincere and well-meaning preachers will continue to quote the Paluxy tracks example as proof that man and dinosaurs lived at the same time.

---

[7] It is beyond the scope of this book to describe the proposed mechanisms creationists use in an attempt to explain how this could have happened. For a well-written and thorough account of how this could be explained according to creationists, a good source would be Walter Brown, *In the Beginning*, (Center for Scientific Creation, Phoenix, Arizona, 1995). In this book, Brown does a better than average job, compared to most creationist literature, of quoting other authors fairly and honestly. The entire book is on-line at www.creationscience.com.

[8] For example, Ronnie J. Hastings, *The Rise and Fall of the Paluxy Mantracks*, Perspectives on Science and Christian Faith, Vol 40, 1988, pp. 144-154, and other references alluded to in this article.

[9] Henry M. Morris, *Scientific Creationism* (Creation Life Publishers, El Cajon, California, 1974), p. 122.

Unfortunately, despite its being disproved, preachers and creationists and just plain misinformed people will quote this supposed evidence as proof that geologists have it all wrong.[10]

The conclusion, then, from the evidence of the alluvial layers on the earth is that the earth appears to be millions of years old at least. Does this prove (in the most comprehensive sense of the word) that the earth is millions of years old? This is an important question to be asked at this point. The answer is no. God certainly could have created the earth out of nothing with an appearance of age. When Jesus fed five thousand people, as recorded in John 6:1-15, he created fish which not only had an appearance of age, but which was ready to be eaten. Bear in mind, however, that if this were true, it would amount to a belief, not a scientific theory. Science, by its very nature, cannot predict or explain a supernatural event.

Did God create the world with an appearance or age? Did he do it in a way analogous to the fish created out of nothing recorded in the sixth chapter of John? If a person would answer yes they should be aware that this conclusion would not be a "scientific" one. It would be based on faith rather than fact. In fact, if God did create the earth with an appearance of age, there would be scientific evidence of age, not youth.

If someone believes that a few thousand years ago God created the earth with an appearance of age, there are implications which should be considered. In that case the fossils buried deep within the earth must have been created right along with the earth. For example, it would imply that dinosaurs, trilobites and a host of other species, which appear in the deeper fossil layers, would never have actually lived at all. In that case, it would almost appear as if God were tricking us by putting into the ground the fossils of animals and plants which never lived. The appearance of age theory will be discussed further in chapter five.

DATING TECHNIQUES

Since the creationists claim the mass of evidence supports the belief that the earth appears young, one might think that they have a large body of evidence to underpin this view. The fact is that their

---

[10] A concise summary of "mantrack" claims and a reasonable refutation is contained in Alan Hayward, *Creation and Evolution* (Bethany House Publishers, Minneapolis Minnesota, 1995), pp. 149-151.

primary means of approach is to attempt to poke holes one at a time in all the evidence for an old earth. They have virtually no empirical evidence they can point to which can be used to say, "look, here is hard evidence that the earth is just a few thousand years old." For example, they will draw into question the accuracy of uranium dating, which is used for estimating the age of what are supposedly some of the oldest rocks in the earth's crust. Perhaps they have a good point. Maybe uranium dating might even be off by 90%. The accuracy and reliability of uranium isotope dating is a technical matter, but even if one could assume that uranium dating could be off by as much as 90%, rocks quoted as being two billion years old would still be 200 million years old. The question remains, what scientific evidence exists for a young earth? Two hundred million years is still a lot older that seven thousand years!

Consider one more example of the kind of evidence used in many creationist writings to support the earth being only a few thousand years old. This evidence has to do with measurements of the amount of certain ions in the oceans. The argument involves measuring the concentration of certain ions in the waters of the ocean. For example, scientists have measured the concentration of sodium in the ocean (sodium is a component of salt). By calculating the total sodium content of the ocean, and by approximating the rate at which sodium enters the ocean at the present day, one could estimate the time it would take for the amount of salt now there to have accumulated, and therefore, perhaps, an estimate of the age of the ocean. There are a lot of difficulties with the accuracy of the numbers, such as the assumption of the flow being constant and so forth, but if one will take the accuracy of the numbers with a grain of salt (No pun intended!), they may reach some sort of useful conclusion. Quoting from a table in one of the creationist publications:[11]

Ocean Ion	Implied Age of the Earth
Sodium	260,000,000 yrs
Chloride	164,000,000 yrs
Lead	2,000 yrs
Nickel	9,000 yrs

[11] Henry M. Morris and Gary E. Parker, *What is Creation Science?*, (Master Books, El Cajon, California, 1987), pp. 288-291.

This table is excerpted from a much longer table. The lead and nickel numbers seem to the untrained to be evidence that the earth is young. In fact, this is simply not the case. As any student of introductory chemistry learns, lead and nickel carbonate are only very slightly soluble. It just so happens that there is a considerable concentration of carbonate in the ocean. The small amount of lead and nickel in the ocean is not due to a young earth, rather it is due to precipitation of the relatively insoluble compounds lead and nickel carbonate (precipitation of other insoluble lead and nickel compounds may also be a factor). The famous white cliffs of Dover are formed of mainly calcium carbonate precipitated in this way. On the other hand, sodium and chloride are quite soluble ions, which could build up to a much higher level in the oceans. Therefore, data of this type seems to imply that the earth appears to be hundreds of millions of years old, not several thousand years. This is true because the numbers in the table represent a minimum age of the ocean, not a maximum age.

Again, does this prove that the oceans are hundreds of millions of years old? No it does not. God could have created the oceans with salt in them. Did he? The reader should decide for themselves. However the one thing can be said with confidence is that from this date the oceans *appear* to be very, very old.

It would be fair to ask at this point why knowledgeable scientists would use "evidence" such as that quoted above to support the contention that the earth appears to be quite young. This is not a question of a simple mistake. Any trained chemist, physicist or, in the case of Henry Morris, geologist, would be well aware that this data supports an old-earth theory. Why would someone put it forth to untrained readers as backing a young-earth theory? This is further support for the contention that if someone approaches a question with their mind already made up about the answer, they will inevitably fall into the trap of bending, sifting and contorting the data in order to reach their pre-conceived conclusion.

Aside from the methods of dating the earth or the universe mentioned above, there exist many other techniques. These include the amount of volcanic rock on the surface of the earth, radioactive decay of potassium, meteoric dust on the moon, optical rotation of biomolecules and so forth. From the cooling of the crust, the earth has been estimated to be two to four billion years old. From the salinity of the oceans, the earth has been estimated at between one and seven billion years old. From radioactive decay of unstable isotopes, it has been estimated to be between two and four and one-half billion years old. From theories about the origin of the moon and loss of kinetic energy of the moon due to tides, it has been estimated to be three to four billion years old. When taken together and analyzed carefully, the data tends to point to an age of the earth of about four and one-half billion years.

It would be appropriate to point out that scientists have had a tendency to be overconfident in trying to give exact numbers for the age of the earth. Nevertheless, although all these methods do not give identical answers, all known data we have imply an age for the earth, the solar system, and the universe of billions of years. I leave the reader with two possible conclusions, both of which agree with the facts as we know them. Either the universe is very old, or it was created more recently in some supernatural way with an appearance of great age. Let the reader decide.

Do not be deceived. Many who would hold the Bible to be inspired by God are convinced not only that the Bible teaches the earth to be very young, but that the weight of scientific evidence supports this claim. Many teachers and preachers in churches quote from creationists or from others who have heard or read materials produced by creationists about the scientific "proof" of the young earth. There is no proof that the earth is young. Dinosaurs did not live at the same time as people! If the reader finds it difficult to accept what is admittedly a rather strong conclusion, then they should make the effort to check out the writings of the creationists for themselves.[12]

Where is the data to support the young-earth or the young-universe theory? Just because people with legitimate Ph.D. degrees claim to believe in this idea does not legitimize their theories. Only empirical evidence can. Much of traditional creationism is simply pseudo-science. It contains claims without proof.

This argument could be taken one step further. Do not be

---

[12] Again, I would refer the reader to the book by Walt Brown mentioned above for several reasons. It is well written and relatively objective. Brown tends to avoid sarcasm and unreasonable out-of-context quotations. Also, it is a fairly recent publication with a great number of references, which can provide access to the literature for those so inclined. The website including the entire book is at www.creationscience.com

deceived. Creationism as taught by some can be dangerous to the faith of those who believe in the Bible. Consider a young student of the sciences who was raised being told that creationism is legitimate science, and that the truth of the Bible is strongly supported by it. That student would surely have their faith sorely tested when they carefully considered what they were learning in their geology, chemistry or biology classes. This student would not be questioning the Bible because their teacher was an atheist, hell-bent to subvert belief in God. In this situation, they would be questioning the Bible simply because in the long run, a deception has a way of being shown for what it is in the clear light of the truth, even if it comes from a sincere religious person.

Once one sees the gaping holes in creationism, where can they put their faith? What about the biblical account of creation? Please hang in there. The Genesis account will be dealt with in greater detail in chapter five. Remember in the meantime that an all-powerful God certainly could have created the earth or in fact the whole universe in an instant with an appearance of great age. The question remains, did God or did he not create the earth with an appearance of age?

Now that I believe I have shown the fallacy of the extreme creationists' view, I would like to move on to deal with the atheists' approach to the data. This will be accomplished in chapters three and four. It will be shown that although subtler, the atheistic view, taken to its logical conclusion, requires dealing with the science in ways somewhat similar to those of the creationists. Remember that if a person approaches a question with a pre-conceived answer in mind, they will somehow manage to fit the data to their answer.

FOR TODAY

1. How old do you think the earth is? ("I am not sure" is a legitimate answer.)

2. Does it matter how old the earth is?

3. What does the claim that the earth was created with an appearance of age mean?

4. How would you explain the "sedimentary rock" layers that are thousands of feet deep at many locations around the earth?

5. In this chapter, the creationists view is described as a fallacy, which is a nice way of saying it is a lie. How does this claim make you feel?

RECOMMENDATION

Decide to read a book written by a creationist as well as one written by an atheist on this general subject.

*[We should] reject all fixed
presuppositions about nature—to
approach natural phenomenon with
a free and unconditional mind.*

Francis Bacon

3

DID THE UNIVERSE JUST HAPPEN?

Does God exist? Does science have anything to say on this matter? Some would insist that the existence of God is a question for theologians to discuss—that it is an irrelevant subject for the practitioners of science. To quote from Niles Eldredge:

> The nineteenth century scientists who were true creationists took both their faith and their interpretation of nature from the Bible, and there never has been any other source of inspiration or support for the "creation model."[1]

Eldredge asserts that there is no evidence whatsoever to support the claim that life or the universe itself were created. He believes one can choose to accept the Bible and all its nice little stories, but there is no actual reason to believe in it. There are two possibilities. Either God exists, or he does not. Simply assuming that God does not exist or saying his existence is irrelevant would be a very ineffective way of making him go away if God were real. An open-minded person, even if they were coming from an atheist background, ought to accept at least the possibility that God exists. If in fact God exists, there would be evidence of that fact in the nature of the universe he created. For Eldredge and other atheists to assert that there is no

---

[1] Niles Eldredge, *The Monkey Business* (Washington Square Press, New York, 1982), p. 142.

evidence for God and leave it at that is intellectually dishonest. In this chapter, some of this evidence will be presented.

Some atheists would like to create the impression that belief in God is for the unintelligent or the superstitious. Try as they might to imply this, the facts show something quite different. Without exception, the great men of the early history of science were believers in God. Copernicus, the first modern scientist to propose the sun to be the center of the solar system, was a deeply religious man who believed God set the celestial bodies in orderly motion. Galileo, despite his run-ins with the Catholic hierarchy, believed that order in the universe demonstrated the existence of God. To quote from Galileo:

> The phenomenon of nature proceed...from the divine Word.

> The glory and greatness of Almighty God are marvelously discerned in all His works and divinely read in the open book of heaven.

> I think in the first place, that it is very pious to say and prudent to confirm that the Holy Bible can never speak untruth—whenever its true meaning is understood.[2]

Johannes Keppler, the scientist who first derived mathematical relationships to describe the motions of the planets, asteroids and comets as elliptical orbits around the sun, was a zealous believer in God. He wrote an interesting book entitled *The Music of the Spheres*, in which he described his view that the harmonious motion of the planets describes a musical symphony created by God. Robert Boyle, the first modern chemist and the first to do careful scientific measurements, was also a theologian who wrote Bible commentaries and religious novels. Priestly, Newton, Linnaeus, Harvey, Cavendish, and Einstein were all believers in God. In fact the belief that science and atheism are compatible is a relatively recent phenomenon, only becoming common about the middle of the nineteenth century.

To quote Melvin Calvin, an atheist and winner of the Nobel prize in chemistry:

---

[2] Excerpts from Galileo's letter to the Grand Duchess Christina in 1614.

> The Fundamental Conviction that the universe is ordered is the first and strongest tenet [of science]. As I try to discern the origin of that conviction, I seem to find it in a basic notion discovered 2000 or 3000 years ago, and enunciated first in the Western world by the ancient Hebrews: namely, that the universe is governed by a single God, and is not the product of the whims of many gods, each governing his own province according to his own laws. This monotheistic view seems to be the historical foundation for modern science.[3]

In other words, Calvin is admitting that the invention of science and the scientific method was due to the Christian belief in a God of order: the God of the Bible. The earliest scientists were all believers in the Bible. They had the conviction that a single God would have created orderly, predictable natural laws. When they sought out these laws, they found them.

These scientists saw God working in the laws of nature. The next step, then, is to look at what is known about the universe to see if this view holds up. What does the nature of the universe as revealed by scientific study have to say about the existence of God?

The argument begins with one assumption.[4] With any argument, one must look carefully at the assumptions. In this case, the underlying assumption which will be made is that the universe exists. That is not a hard assumption to buy. Although philosophers may argue about whether a tree, when it falls to the earth in a place where nobody hears it, makes a sound, we all know that it does. In fact, we could record the sound on tape.

Given that the universe exists, there are two possibilities which follow from this assumption. Either the universe has always existed or it has not. If it has always existed, then it was not created. If it has not always existed, then the universe was created. A thing cannot create itself. Physicists and philosophers call this the law of causality. Since the universe could not create itself (cause itself to exist), that would imply some sort of creator. The argument could be outlined in

[3] Melvin Calvin, *Chemical Evolution* (Oregon State System of Higher Education, Eugene, Oregon, 1961), p. 258.

[4] Although the details of the argument in chapter three are mine, I would acknowledge the outline of the argument was inspired by the work of John Clayton, a lecturer as well as the author of a number of articles on the subject. Clayton's Website is www.doesgodexist.org

the following figure:

Assumption: The Universe Exists.

Therefore the universe has either:

1) Always Existed

OR

2) Not Always Existed

In other words, therefore, the universe has either:

1) Not Been Created

OR

2) Been Created

If it was created, then there is a creator. The outline of the argument is very simple. The skeptic could protest use of the word created as too suggestive, but any synonym used would still imply that the universe was created.

Has the universe always existed? What is the history of the universe? For simplicity, consider three possible explanations.

1. The Steady State Theory.
2. The Big Bang Theory.
3. Creation with an appearance of age.

THE STEADY STATE THEORY

We will consider the steady state theory first. This theory, simply put, involves the belief that the universe has always existed.

According to this theory, the laws of nature which may be observed by scientists, have been in effect for all time and will be in effect in the exact same form forever. Actually, it would be more accurate to refer to the steady state theories, as various forms have been propounded over the years.

The earliest steady state theorists held to the idea that all matter and energy have existed forever. The processes observable to us at the present time have always been occurring. All that can happen is that the matter and energy of the universe can be redistributed. This theory does not require the existence of a creator. It was therefore a natural product of the budding atheistic philosophy of the nineteenth century, intent on finding a non-supernatural explanation for the existence of the universe. It is worth noting that virtually all scientists as well as western philosophers up until well into the nineteenth century accepted as fact both creation and a creator, seemingly without serious question.

It was not just atheistic thinking which motivated scientists to ask new questions about the nature of the origin of the universe, however. With discoveries such as that of Sir William Herschell in the late eighteenth century that some of the nebulae observable in the sky are actually other galaxies besides our own Milky Way, it became clear that the universe is of unimaginably vast dimensions. With the discovery of galaxies at a distance of many millions of light years away, it was only natural for scientists to ask how they came to be. Our job is to look at the evidence and the theories proposed to explain that evidence, and to ask whether they are consistent with belief in the creator or not.

Remember, either the universe was created or it was not. The earliest steady state theorists did not actually attempt to explain how the universe came to be. They held to the idea that the universe just is. It has always existed. In other words, it was not created. The problem with this theory as will be shown is that it is in direct contradiction to the laws of nature. In fact, even among atheists, this form of steady state theory is out of favor because it does not hold up to the laws of thermodynamics.

Thermodynamics is the branch of chemistry and physics which deals with the relationships between matter and various forms of energy on a macroscopic scale. It is often summarized in two or three simple "Laws of Thermodynamics." It is in its conflict with these laws that the steady state theories run into trouble. For this reason, these laws will be stated in a fairly simple form to help convey how they relate to the origin of the universe. The first law of thermodynamics might be stated:

> In a closed system, the sum of mass and energy is conserved.

A closed system is one in which matter and energy do not enter or leave. In other words, assuming the universe is in fact a closed system, the amount of mass and energy in it does not change. Types of energy may be interconverted. For example the energy stored in gasoline may be converted to heat and mechanical energy, but the total amount of energy is constant. Einstein, with his famous equation $E=mc^2$, proposed that matter and energy can be interconverted, leading to the development of nuclear energy but also requiring the first law to include both mass and energy in its statement.

How does this relate to the steady state or any other theory of origins? Atheists tend to claim that observable scientific laws discovered in nature and the laboratory can explain all past and present events. This assumption of atheists may or may not be true, but if it is applied to the case of the first law of thermodynamics, then it would require, as the early steady state theorists claimed, that all the matter of the universe has existed forever. According to this view, any supernatural event such as creation would be just a fantasy created by those who are unable to accept the truth.

How does one resolve the question of whether or not the matter and energy of the universe have existed forever? Are the observable facts about the universe consistent with this theory? In order to answer this question, consider a statement of the second law of thermodynamics.

> For any spontaneous process in a closed system, entropy increases.

Unfortunately, the concept of entropy is a bit more abstract than that of energy, but a few examples might help. Entropy can be defined as a measure of randomness or disorder. A messy room has a lot of entropy. Applying the second law to a room in a house (a questionable application to a scientist, but it may help understand the second law), the natural tendency for a room is to go from order to disorder, unless an outside force such as the occupant cleaning it up is applied. A house built out of cards has a lot of order by comparison to a random pile of playing cards. A pile of cards would never spontaneously pick themselves up and build a house, but the slightest gust of wind would naturally blow a house of cards apart.

Entropy has been called "time's arrow" because it can be used to decide the natural forward direction of any process. For example, if a person viewed a film in which a huge cloud of dust and rubble suddenly came together to form a building, they would know beyond a doubt that they were seeing the film in reverse. Using a chemical example, smoke, ash, carbon dioxide and water will never come together spontaneously to create a piece of paper, whereas the reverse process is spontaneous. The second law of thermodynamics will be discussed in some more detail in the Appendix.

How does this law apply to the origin and current state of the universe? Stated simply, the second law of thermodynamics implies that given sufficient time, in the absence of supernatural intervention, the universe will run down completely. Eventually, all the fuel in each of the stars will be used up. The universe will become extremely cold. Ultimately, given enough time, no life could be supported anywhere in the universe.

This fact has dire consequences for the earliest forms of steady state theory. If the universe, including all its matter and energy has always existed, then it should already have reached the logical conclusion of the second law. It should be completely cold and dark. There is no way around this deathblow to the older form of the steady state theory.

Either the universe has always existed, or it has not. If the universe is a closed system, then according to the laws of nature as observable to scientists, it could not have always existed. If it has not always existed, then it was created. The conclusion one is left with, then, is that the universe was created.

Actually, disproving the steady state theory is not quite as simple as that. In 1948, three physicists Hermann Bondi, Thomas Gold and Fred Hoyle devised a new steady state theory, which was startling in its time. They proposed that the universe is not a closed system. In other words they theorized that matter is continuously and spontaneously created right in place in the universe out of nothing! This theory is sometimes called the theory of continuous creation. This theory would seem to eliminate the problem with applying the second law of thermodynamics to the steady state theory. According to the theory of continuous creation, the stuff out of which stars form is created at a continuous although very slow rate spontaneously out of nothing. This would explain why there are still stars around, giving off light and continuously increasing the entropy of the universe. In other words, Hoyle, Gold, Bondi and others proposed that the first law of thermodynamics is not strictly true. Matter and energy are continuously created out of nothing. They claimed that the universe has always existed: that this matter has been in the process of being created forever. As could be imagined, this created quite a stir in the scientific community, which was used to taking the first law as being proven. If matter has been created out of nothing forever, shouldn't there be an infinite amount of matter? Wouldn't this mean the universe would be a lot more crowded?

This question requires the mentioning of one of the greatest discoveries of astronomy in the twentieth century. In 1929, Edwin Hubble published his law of expansion of the universe, using as evidence the red shift of light approaching us from very distant celestial objects.

The "red shift" can be explained using an analogous everyday example. Consider the sound heard when a speeding train or racecar passes by. When the car or train is approaching, the sound heard has a higher pitch, while after it passes, the pitch becomes lower. This is true because when an object is moving toward an observer, it is moving into its own sound waves, making the waves in front of the object closer together than they would have been if the car or train or whatever was not moving. Behind the sound source, the sound waves are actually farther apart. When the object is moving toward an observer, the waves hit more often than they otherwise would have because they are compressed together. A higher frequency or pitch is heard. When the object is receding, the waves hit less often, and a lower pitch is observed.

The same is true for light approaching the earth from distant celestial objects. The colors of the visible light spectrum go from red to orange, yellow, green, blue and violet. It so happens that red light has the lowest frequency while violet light has the highest frequency. A very rapidly receding object is said to be shifted to the red (to lower frequency), while an object approaching the earth at a great speed would be "blue shifted" (to higher frequency). Figure 3.1 provides an explanation of this effect.

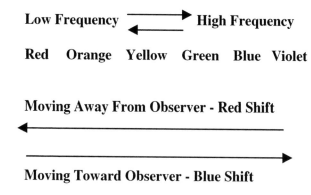

Figure 3.1
The "red shift" implies a light-producing object is moving away from an observer

In 1868, Sir William Huggins was the first to use this principle to determine that the star Sirius is moving away from the sun at 29 miles per second. Some of the stars in the Milky Way galaxy are approaching us, while others are receding. However, when galaxies at a great distance are studied, they are consistently found to be receding. In fact, it is found that the farther away a galaxy or quasar is from our own position, the greater the size of the red shift is observed. Knowledge of this fact led to Hubble's law of universal expansion. The bottom line is that the universe appears to be expanding very rapidly. This will have important consequences when the big bang theory is discussed.

In regard to the steady state theory, if the universe is expanding at a constant rate, then this could explain why the universe is not totally packed with matter, even though matter has been created forever. As unlikely as this theory seems on the face of it, it is logically consistent.

The Steady State/Continuous Creation theory has come to be dismissed by most physicists however. This is true because the theory makes certain predictions which are simply not true. If this theory were correct, then the stars at great distances should be on average of the same age as those near us. Also, if it were true, then the distribution of galaxies should be roughly even. Both of these predictions prove to be incorrect. The stars at a great distance appear to be younger than stars in our own and other nearby galaxies. This is presumably true because the light left these stars so long ago (as much as billions of years), that the light from these distant objects represent a snapshot of the universe when it was much younger. Also, the galaxies are not even close to being distributed evenly throughout space. In fact, the universe contains great clusters of galaxies and even "superclusters" of galaxies. Therefore, the distribution of galaxies is not at all even, as would be predicted by the steady state theory.

The Continuous Creation model runs into another problem for its proponents, intent on creating a model with no necessity for God. How does this matter come into existence out of nothing? Hoyle and others have postulated a "creation field": a sort of creative force in the universe. It sounds an awful lot like they are resorting to a creator to explain the universe! The problem is that there is no evidence to support the existence of this force.

The history of science includes many examples of theories, which have invoked special forces or substances to explain mysterious phenomenon. For example, early scientists proposed that living beings contain a substance called "anima" to explain how they differed from inanimate objects. This substance was never isolated, and later the anima theory was dropped. Flammable substances were theorized to contain "phlogiston"—a substance, which was never isolated or detected in any way. Later, when it was discovered that flammable substances react with oxygen, the phlogiston theory was dropped. As another example, when scientists could not explain how light could pass through the vacuum of space without medium to carry it, they proposed the mysterious substance called "ether" for light to pass through. The ether theory suffered the same fate that the continuous creation model is suffering: it ended up in the theory trash-heap, not because the scientists who proposed them were bad scientists, but because the models were unsupported by scientific measurements.

Where did this theory come from in the first place? Quoting from a cosmologist who has no particular reason to oppose the steady-state theory:

> The basis for acceptance or rejection of the evolutionary [big bang] and steady-state theories can be

divided into two categories: observational (experimental) proof and philosophical reasoning. The evolutionary theory rests heavily on the former, while the greatest appeal of the steady-state theory, at least at the present time, lies not so much in its mathematical formulation and predictions as it does in its broad philosophical implications.[5]

In other words, those who hold to the steady-state theory do so, not so much because any evidence supports the theory, but because they find the idea of creation unacceptable philosophically. It would be fair to say that the truth is still the truth, even if it is not philosophically appealing.

The lack of evidence to support the idea of the universe existing forever explains why most cosmologists now believe in the creation theory commonly known as the big bang theory. Let it be said again, the big bang theory is a creation theory. From personal experience (which is by no means a scientific survey) the author has found that a majority of physicists have at least some sort of belief in God. A look at the big bang theory may provide some of the reason for this.

THE BIG BANG THEORY

The big bang theory was first proposed by George Gamow and a student of his, Ralph Alpher, in 1946. A simple statement defining the theory could be as follows: **At some point in time all the matter and energy in the universe appeared instantaneously at a single point in space**. The initial creation existed as pure energy in the form of photons (particles of light). As the photons expanded at an extremely fast rate, they began to combine to form other high-energy particles. As the created stuff expanded further and cooled, electrons, protons and neutrons were created, which eventually came together as the matter cooled still further to form atoms. Further expansion yielded huge conglomerates of matter—mainly hydrogen and helium, which eventually coalesced into galaxies and discrete stars within those galaxies (apologies to those for whom this description was too

---

[5] James Coleman, *Modern Theories of the Universe* (Signet, New York, 1963). Although this is a somewhat old source for the quote, it would be even truer today with so much more evidence in support of the big bang theory.

technical). See the figure below.

Time	Temperature	Event	Simple View
0 seconds	Infinite	Singularity occurs. Light forms.	
10^{-10} seconds	10^{15} Kelvin	Protons, neutrons and electrons form	
1 second	10^{10} Kelvin	Atomic nuclei begin to form	
3 minutes	10^{9} Kelvin	Atoms begin to form with electrons associated with a nucleus	
1 billion years	3000 Kelvin	Matter has cooled enough that it can coalesce into galaxies and stars	

It would be impossible to prove that this event occurred in the strictest sense of proof, since it presumably happened a very long time ago. Estimates are about 12 to 20 billion years ago. Recent data from the Hubble telescope tends to narrow the estimates to 13-15 billion years ago. Although the theory cannot be proven absolutely, there is a considerable body of evidence to support it. A brief description of that evidence follows.

The first evidence, which supports the big bang theory, is the "red shift," which has already been mentioned. If the universe did indeed begin with one giant explosion, then all the matter would be moving outward from the point of the explosion with a great speed. In this case, all galaxies other than our own would be moving away from us. The farther a galaxy or cluster of galaxies is from the earth, the faster it should be moving away. If this were true, then light reaching the earth from the most distant galaxies, would be shifted to lower frequency than light from a relatively closer galaxy. In fact, this prediction from the big bang theory is in exact agreement with the evidence as mentioned above. The big bang theory was originally proposed as an explanation of the rapidly expanding universe.

Since the big bang theory was formulated, physicists have developed a model, using the laws of physics, to predict the exact nature and history of this bang. In doing so, the models predicted that there should be a fairly weak microwave "background radiation" still echoing throughout the universe. A prediction of both the intensity and frequency of this radiation was made in 1964. When astronomers began to look for this radiation, it was indeed found to be present with about the right intensity and frequency as predicted from the theory.

In 1989, a satellite called the Cosmic Background Explorer measured this radiation with great accuracy, finding the data to fit the big bang model very well. When a theory predicts the existence of a then-unknown phenomenon, after which scientists go out and discover this prediction to be true, this is the strongest kind of support a theory can have. This background radiation provides further very strong supportive evidence that the big bang may actually have occurred.

As a third example of evidence to support the big bang theory, current models of the big bang predict that the original explosion occurred so rapidly that significant amounts of only the lightest elements, mostly hydrogen and helium, would have been created.

Heavier elements such as carbon, nitrogen, iron and so forth would only have been created later inside of stars. The theory predicts certain percentages of hydrogen and helium, which turns out to be in good agreement with observations of interstellar material. Again, the big bang model is able to predict correctly facts about the universe.

If the big bang theory is correct, it would mean that, at some point in time and space, out of nothing an inconceivable amount of light suddenly appeared. This is reminiscent of Genesis 1:3: "And God said 'Let there be light,' and there was light." If this theory of origins is true—and the evidence available supports the theory—then the universe was created by something or someone outside the universe itself. The universe could not have created itself. It was created by a creator. As physicists ponder the big bang theory, they must ask themselves what caused it all to happen. What force created all this light? The name that has been given to this "force," this creator, is God. In his book *Kinematic Relativity*, E. A. Milne, who never referred to divinity in the entire book, concludes it by saying: "The first cause of the universe is left for the reader to insert, But our picture is incomplete without Him."

It would be worth reiterating that this does not prove that the universe was created with a big bang. In fact, in the case of theories about events of the distant past, scientists will remain unable to provide absolute proof. Scientific discovery must always remain tentative, pending further study. This is especially true when trying to explain events which occurred a long, time ago, and therefore are not subject to direct experiment. In conclusion, in the light of scientific evidence and the laws of science, the idea that the universe has always existed—that there was no creator—has been shown to be false. Although one cannot say with certainty that the big bang happened, the evidence scientists have thus far collected is in dramatic agreement with this theory: a theory that implies the universe was created out of nothing.

CREATION WITH AN APPEARANCE OF AGE

This leads to the last theory of the origin of the universe to be considered. This is the theory that God created the universe with an appearance of age. The God one can read about in the Bible certainly could have created planets, stars, galaxies, and super-clusters of galaxies in place out of nothing. In fact, he might have done it only a few thousand years ago. It should be noted that this would be an unfalsifiable theory. If the universe was created with an appearance of age, then there would not necessarily be any direct scientific evidence to either support or disprove the youth of the universe. This theory would be consistent with a simple and literal interpretation of the first chapter of Genesis, but by the very nature of this theory, no one could ever prove or disprove it using science. It is essentially a non-scientific theory.

Certainly atheists would be uncomfortable with this concept. They assume, before even looking at the evidence, that the origins of the universe has a "natural" explanation. However, the creation of the universe, whether by the big bang or with an appearance of age is a supernatural event.

Which of the three proposed theories is true: steady state, big bang or appearance of age? It can be shown that the steady state theory, the one consistent with atheism, is insupportable. Between the other two, it will be left to the reader to decide. As a scientist, I confess that I am pulled toward the "scientific" theory. As a science teacher, when I lecture on astronomy, I usually only spend significant time on the big bang theory because it is the only "scientific" theory in agreement with the evidence. By faith, I believe God could have created an expanding universe with the background radiation already echoing through it, but this would be a belief based on faith, not measurable fact. Since neither theory can be proven, it would be a mistake to be dogmatic in condemning the big bang theory or the theory of creation with an appearance of age.

To conclude, the very existence of the universe as we know it shows that there is a creator. The nature of the universe does not tell a lot about this creator except that he is certainly very powerful. Whether this creator is a personal god or not is not made obvious by the mere existence of the universe and the laws which govern it. In the next chapter, by looking at the nature of life, we will learn a bit more about the nature of the creator.

FOR TODAY

1. How do you believe the universe came to be?

2. Do you believe the big bang occurred?

3. Do you believe that faith in God is a form of superstition? Why or why not?

4. According to the chapter, how do we know the universe has not always existed?

5. What does the existence of the universe—of stars, galaxies, planets and so forth—say about the nature of its creator?

No way of thinking, no matter how ancient, should be accepted without proof.

Thoreau

4

DID LIFE JUST HAPPEN?

What about the life that exists on the earth? How can one explain the origin of hundreds of thousands of species of plants, as well as insects, reptiles, birds, mammals, and most complex of all, humans? To the Christian, although all this life is a thing of beauty and wonder, the explanation is no problem. As Jesus said in Matthew 3:9, "I tell you that out of these stones God can raise up children for Abraham." The Bible believer accepts this claim of Jesus without difficulty. They would believe that God could take the matter in rocks and make living, breathing adults out of them. He could do it even though the elemental composition of the material in the rocks is not of the right proportion to create organic matter. God could do that. In fact, Christians would believe that Jesus could have made children for Abraham out of nothing at all.

In the Bible it is recorded that Jesus turned water into wine at a wedding feast (John 2:1-11). He created fish and bread out of nothing in order to feed several thousand people at once (John 6:1-15). When a person who believes these Biblical accounts looks at the astounding variety and beauty of nature, the source of it all is obvious. It was created by God. However, this argument will probably not be convincing to the skeptic or the atheist.

To the atheist, the existence of all this life is equally a thing of beauty and wonder. The explanation is more problematic, however. He or she believes that every observable phenomenon has a natural explanation, based on the laws of nature. How such an incredible phenomenon as a living organism could just happen by accident surely is a notion awesome to contemplate, but the atheist is sure there is a natural explanation. For the atheist, it is simply a matter of searching and searching until the scientific explanation for how life came to be is found. The question to be asked in this chapter is whether or not this "natural" explanation is real or just an illusion.

The second argument for the existence of God begins with a simple assumption. It will be assumed that life exists. (In case you are not sure, feel free to pinch yourself now) Probably this assumption will not be greatly debated. It has already been shown that life has not always existed. This is true because if the universe has not always existed, then surely life has not always existed either. The question, then, is how did life come about? Two possible explanations present themselves. Either life was created by someone or something, or it occurred by some natural process (to quote from Julian Huxley again, it "just happened"). The first explanation requires the existence of some supernatural power—what we call God. The second explanation would be consistent with the atheist view. To outline this argument:

Assumption: Life Exists.

Therefore life was either:

1)   Created.

OR

2) It Just Happened.

Which implies either:

1)   There Is A Creator.

OR

2)   There Is No Creator.

The attempts to explain the existence of life using scientific knowledge will be considered first. There exists a sub-branch of science dealing with questions of the chemistry of the origins of life. The most famous experiment quoted by scientists in the field is that of Urey and Miller, performed in 1953 and published in *Science*.[1] In this experiment, Urey and Miller prepared a mixture of methane (CH_4), water (H_2O), ammonia (NH_3) and hydrogen (H_2) in a glass vessel. They then proceeded to apply an electric spark to the mixture and analyzed the liquid which precipitated out of the mixture. Upon analyzing the reaction mixture, they found that it contained amino acids. These are fairly small molecules, although more complex than the four substances which made up the original mixture. This result was seen by Urey and Miller to be important, because amino acids are the building block molecules out of which proteins are synthesized.

Urey and Miller proposed that the early atmosphere of the earth might have been made out of water, methane, ammonia and hydrogen, and that this might be the first step in explaining how the protein molecules in the first spontaneously generated life came to be. This experiment has been cited as the first great discovery on the path toward explaining how life came to be. In an article in the popular *Parade* magazine, Carl Sagan referred to this experiment.

> From the standpoint of a 19th-century biologist, the achievement of experiments like Urey and Miller's is stunning.[2]

Sagan proceeds to quote from Darwin:

> "It is mere rubbish thinking at present of the origin of life," wrote Charles Darwin. "One might as well think of the origin of matter." How amazed he would be today! There is still much to do. No one has performed such an experiment and, at the end, discovered a creature, however simple, crawling out of the test tube. Many mysteries remain. We don't know how early nucleic acids "instructed" the

---

[1] S. L. Miller, "Production of Amino Acids Under Possible Primitive Earth Conditions," *Science*, Vol. 117 (1953), p. 528.

[2] Carl Sagan, "How Life Began," *Parade*, December 2, 1984.

formation of early proteins (a problem called the origin of the genetic code). We don't understand the origin of the first cell...There are scientists who are dazzled by our deep ignorance of many phases of this subject, who despair of our ever understanding its more complex aspects and who look longingly toward extraterrestrial *or even divine intervention* (emphasis mine).

But such ideas do not solve the problem of the origin of life; they merely postpone having to deal with it. While by no means underestimating the depth of our ignorance, I am amazed by how much we've learned. Understanding the origin of life no longer seems intractable. The progress begun by Urey and Miller stands as a landmark of modern science and our understanding of the universe and ourselves.

This lengthy quote from Sagan is given both to give the feel for the mindset of atheists, and to provide an example of their line of thinking which can be referred to later. Notice that, as Sagan quotes him, Darwin believed the creation of life as well as of the universe was beyond the realm of science. In fact, Darwin made a rather interesting statement in his original 1859 edition of *Origin of Species*. To quote:

Therefore I should infer from analogy that probably all the organic beings which have ever lived upon this earth have descended from one primordial form into which life was first breathed by the Creator.

Was the discovery of Urey and Miller a "landmark in our understanding of the universe" as claimed by Sagan? The answer is an emphatic no. As an organic chemist, I could have predicted before they did the experiment that an electrolyzed mixture of methane, ammonia and water with a little hydrogen would produce a very low concentration of amino acids. Amino acids are very stable molecules over the short run. It could also have been predicted that if Urey and Miller continued to add the spark and heat, the amino acids concentration would have eventually been greatly diminished, leaving behind a polymerized mess that organic chemists affectionately call "tar" in the bottom of the flask. Although it was a nice experiment, this was no great discovery at all, because it led to results that any organic chemist would have predicted beforehand. The question is not whether amino acids could have been produced in some model early atmosphere. The question is whether this is a significant step toward explaining how life came to exist on our planet.

What are Carl Sagan and others like him really claiming? They are claiming that the chemical environment on the ancient earth allowed the right combination of molecules to spontaneously come together and produce a living thing. It would be worth while to go into some detail explaining what would be required in order for this event, if it happened, to occur.

All living things (and presumably the first life) are composed of four classes of molecules: proteins, nucleic acids, carbohydrates and lipids. Proteins are very large molecules made up of many amino acid molecules bonded together. Proteins molecules are responsible for digestion, nutrient transport, energy production, immune system function, blood clotting, and an innumerable number of other functions in any living thing. Enzymes, the chemical factories in cells, are an example of a type of protein molecules.

Nucleic acids are huge polymeric molecules formed out of nitrogen containing bases called purines and pyrimidines, connected to one another through a backbone of sugar and phosphate units. DNA (deoxyribose nucleic acid) is responsible for heredity in all living things. The discovery of its double alpha helical structure, much like a spiral staircase, by Watson and Crick was one of the greatest discoveries in the history of science. Nucleic acids in the form of RNA (ribose nucleic acid) are also responsible for the synthesis of proteins.

Carbohydrates are a third category of biological molecules. They are commonly known as sugars. They are mostly smaller molecules whose main function is as a source of energy. Although this is the primary function of sugars, they are also involved in a large number of other biological functions. For example, sugars are one of the components of nucleic acids as mentioned above. Cellulose, the main component in plant cell walls, is a sugar polymer.

Lipids are a broad class of non-water-soluble molecules. Examples would include fats, a primary source of energy, and steroids such as cholesterol. Many steroids are hormones, regulating numerous biological functions such as reproduction.

The atheist's theory requires the conditions for production of all four types of compounds to have existed on the primeval earth. In fact, purines and pyrimidines, the building blocks of nucleic acids have been created in a separate experiment somewhat like that of Urey and Miller. However, the primitive atmosphere required for this experiment contained different molecules from those required to produce proteins. Carbohydrates have also been created in a different "primitive atmosphere." The conditions under which carbohydrates can be spontaneously generated require a strongly oxidizing (oxygen-containing) atmosphere, while the conditions required for the production of amino acids require a strongly reducing (hydrogen-containing) atmosphere. The problem is that these two types of primitive atmospheric conditions are logical opposites. Scientists to this day debate whether the early atmosphere of the earth was reducing or not. One thing they would presumably be unanimous on is that it was not both reducing and oxidizing at the same time because the two are logical opposites!

Which is the right atmosphere? Which one actually existed? The one which would allow amino acids would not allow carbohydrates or nucleic acids to occur. To date, no primitive atmospheric conditions have been proposed under which lipid molecules such as fats or steroids have been shown to be produced spontaneously in significant concentrations. Even if this discovery were made, however, it would not change the problem for the atheist trying to propose how the ancient atmosphere of the earth could create these very different types of molecules.

Let it be granted that the earth could have four different atmospheres or at least four different environments in four different places (as unlikely as that seems). Let it be said that amino acids could be produced in one ocean, nucleic acids could be produced in another, and carbohydrates in still another. Where lipids could be spontaneously created, it would be hard to say, but for now let it just be granted that lipid molecules could be spontaneously produced somewhere on the earth. After this, all four of the basic types of building block chemicals would have to somehow float great distances from where they were created, and meet up somewhere. At this meeting point, all these molecules would have to exist in sufficient concentrations and the right proportions to allow the formation of a living thing, despite the fragility of even some of these building block molecules.

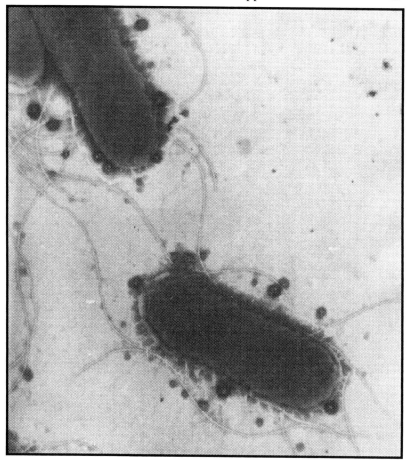

Figure 4.1 An electron micrograph of two E. coli with another coming into the top left of the photo.

Please consider this theory even more closely. For the moment, let it be assumed that somehow amino acids, nucleic acids, carbohydrates and lipids could all simultaneously be produced at different points and find their way together (as unlikely as that seems). Even if a "soup" containing all four types of molecules, even in the correct proportions were to come together by some seemingly inconceivable process, that soup would be far from being able to produce life—very far. In fact, it would never happen. What would be the requirements to allow the simplest living thing to be viable? The simplest living thing would have to be able to:

1. Recognize, ingest and digest food.
2. Turn that food into usable energy.
3. Grow.
4. Reproduce.

It would probably have to be able to move as well. Bacteria are the simplest known form of life which passes this test. Therefore, they will be used for comparison. Viruses are simpler, but they are much too simple to live on their own. They can only exist as parasites on more complex living things. One of the simplest types of bacteria is *E. coli*. Consider *E. coli* as a model for the simplest possible life form. *E. coli* are about one micrometer by three micrometers (0.001 by 0.003 mm) in size. They contain approximately 7×10^{11} atoms (that is about seven hundred billion atoms!)

The single cell of an E. coli contains about three thousand different protein molecules, fifty different carbohydrate molecules, forty different lipid molecules and 1000 different nucleic acid molecules, as well as about five hundred other simple organic molecules which do not fit into any of the above categories. The skeptic could debate this model. They could claim that the first spontaneous life form could contain only one hundred billion atoms, two thousand different protein molecules and so forth. This would not change any of the arguments or conclusions below.

Consider for a moment the amazing level of the complexity of this simplest life form, which supposedly was created by a natural chemical process. For example, consider one of the basic categories of molecules: proteins. Proteins are extremely large and complex molecules. A model of what is a relatively very simple protein molecule is given in Figure 4.2 as an example of the complexity of protein molecules.

As another example of a protein molecule, consider hemoglobin (not a protein molecule actually present in bacteria, but one which most readers have probably heard of). The formula of hemoglobin is $C_{2952}H_{4664}O_{832}N_{812}S_8Fe_4$. Each of the over nine thousand atoms must be connected in exactly the right order for hemoglobin to work. Not only that, but every atom must be in exactly the correct geometric orientation with respect to all the others in order for hemoglobin to function. This protein consists of four separate chains, each containing 146 amino acids. Sickle cell anemia

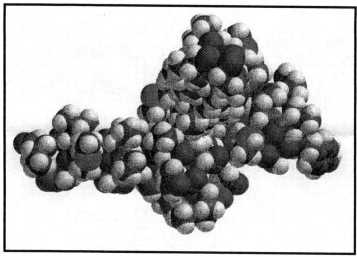

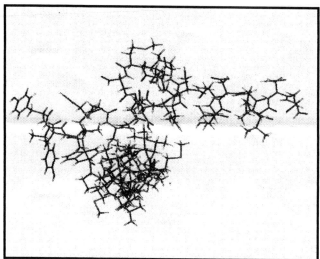

Figure 4.2. A model of a very simple protein molecule, representing both the size and the geometric complexity of protein molecules.

is caused by replacing just one of the 146 amino acids with another one. Urey and Miller may have shown that some of the twenty naturally occurring amino acids in proteins could be synthesized in some sort of model atmosphere. This is a huge leap from showing how actual protein molecules with biological activity could form, to say the least. Notice that any protein molecule has to be composed of twenty different amino acids. It is extremely unlikely, in fact one might claim it would be impossible, for any environment to spontaneously produce all twenty amino acids in a proportion which would allow even a single protein molecule to be produced. Besides, any other amino acid molecules (outside the twenty which occur in proteins) which were spontaneously created would have to be excluded from the proteins in the first living thing. It is extremely difficult to see how this could happen spontaneously.

The problem of making a biologically active protein molecule is even more immense. There is even another level of impossibility layered on top of the three impossibilities just described (formation of four types of biological molecules, formation of all twenty amino acids, combination of those twenty into a biologically active molecule). In order to discuss this, the structure of nucleic acids must be described first.

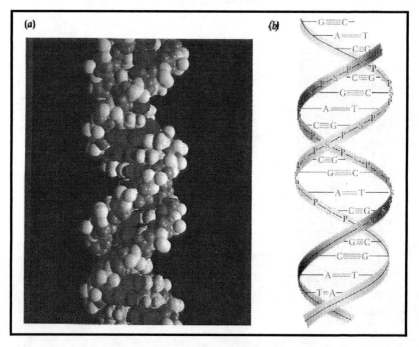

Figure 4.3. Figure (a) on the left shows all of the atoms in a small portion of the double-helical structure of DNA. Figure (b) on the right shows the same portion of the molecule schematically. S = ribose sugar molecule, P = phosphate group, and C, A, G and T represent purine and pyrimidine molecules.

Nucleic acids, the material out of which genes are composed, like proteins, are extremely complex molecules. A picture of one small proportion of a single strand of DNA is given in Figure 4.3.

DNA, as discovered by Watson and Crick, has a beautiful "double-helical" structure. A DNA molecule is a template which cells use to manufacture proteins. The process by which this occurs, involving RNA as well as a number of protein molecules, is very complex—beyond the scope of this book. In order for life to have formed spontaneously, a large number of different nucleic acid molecules, all with the correct double helical structure would have had to form simultaneously in the same place. Not only that, but each of these DNA molecules would have needed to be able to successfully manufacture protein molecules able to ingest and metabolize food, to regulate nutrient levels in the cell, and to perform thousands of different tasks in the cell.

The formation of all these DNA molecules by random association of the accidentally formed soup of chemicals would involve a lot of coincidence, to say the least. In fact, the probability of even one useful DNA molecule forming spontaneously is essentially zero as will be shown. Not only this, but there is a logical impossibility built into this supposed formation of the first cell by accident. In living things, the formation of DNA molecules requires protein molecules called enzymes, while the synthesis of the enzymes required to form the DNA molecules in the first place requires the existence of DNA molecules (See Figure 4.4).

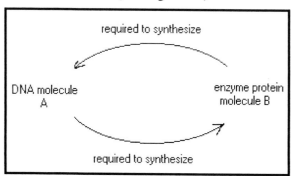

Figure 4.4. An illogical pair of simultaneously created molecules. Two classes of molecules, both of which require the other in order to be synthesized. Which came first, DNA or enzymes?

Which came first, the chicken or the egg? The atheist, of course, will answer that they both were formed at the same time. Now that is amazing! The atheist would claim that DNA molecule A, required to synthesize enzyme B, was spontaneously formed by a chemical accident. The problem with this is that enzyme molecule B might be one of the proteins required for DNA molecule A to be synthesized. This creates an apparent logical impossibility, represented by the Figure 4.4.

Both of the uniquely paired molecules would have to be created simultaneously by accident, even though both are required to synthesize their partner. That would be an unbelievable coincidence.

The atheist theory of how life came to exist requires that all three thousand of these almost unimaginably complex and delicate biologically active protein molecules required for the first living cell to function and reproduce itself all just happen to be created in the same place at the same time. Not only that, but one thousand different nucleic acid molecules would also have to show up in exactly the same place—and not just any nucleic acids—ones capable of synthesizing the correct proteins to produce an active cell which can eat, grow, and reproduce. The problem of lipids and carbohydrates has not even yet been discussed, never mind the five hundred "other molecules" in the model *E. coli* cell.

One would think that scientists who believe life "just happened" would have a theory to explain from the laws of nature how all these incredibly complex molecules came to exist and managed to coalesce into a living thing. This leap in the theory from production of the simple amino acids, purines, pyrimidines and carbohydrates to the supermolecules such as proteins, DNA, RNA and so forth is one place where the scientists are really grasping at straws. A quote from the book, *Evolution and Christian Thought Today*, by Hearn and Hendry can give a feel for what believers in the spontaneous generation of life would say at this point.

It now seems reasonable to believe that the earth's early atmosphere and the constitution of its crust favored the formation of organic compounds, at least locally, and that over the long periods of pre-biological time very large amounts of chemical energy were accumulated in this way.

It seems highly possible, although still not clearly

demonstrated, that natural forces existed which would have favored the formation of highly complex molecules and aggregates of such molecules, and that the chemical structures of such complexes could have had some ability to catalyze certain types of chemical reactions. If any of the reactions catalyzed were more favorable to the synthesis of the catalyst than others, a mechanism such as *natural selection* could begin operating, even at this pre-biological level. Gradually, this process could conceivably lead to increased catalytic efficiency, given the randomness characteristic of molecular interactions and *sufficient time*. It also seems likely that many of the metabolic reactions of modern living things could have arisen separately in these pre-living complexes, and that a complete metabolic machine may have appeared only after long periods of *chemical evolution* of such systems.[3] (emphasis mine)

This quote is from one of the earlier books on the subject, but it accurately relates the heart of every theory of how this first life form "just happened." This quote points out three elements necessary in any "scientific" explanation of the origin of life.

1. Natural selection of molecules.
2. Chemical evolution.
3. Sufficient time.

Is it reasonable for scientists to believe that molecules can undergo natural selection? Can non-living chemicals evolve over time into more and more complex molecules? Have these processes been observed in the laboratory? Do they agree with the known laws of science? The answer in each case is an emphatic no! A magic ingredient in this formula is "sufficient time." Does sufficient time increase the probability of this happening? Again, the well-known laws of nature, which any scientist is quite aware of, say no.

In order to answer the above question, refer back to the second law of thermodynamics. This law governs what types of processes can and cannot happen. Processes which result in a net decrease in entropy of a system and its environment do not happen. Natural

---

[3] Walter Hearn and Richard Henry, *Evolution and Christian Thought Today* (Paternoster, London, 1959), p. 66,67.

processes proceed from order to disorder. Proteins and nucleic acids are molecules with an extreme amount of order. This would be especially true of a protein or nucleic acid capable of some sort of biological activity. The probability of a single active strand of DNA, which would be called a gene, being produced by accident out of a solution, even if it contained some sort of ideal mixture of purines, pyrimidines, deoxyribose sugar molecules and phosphate is essentially zero. The probability of thousands of different active nucleic acid molecules being produced together in one place is zero twice over (this is not exactly good scientific terminology, but hopefully the point is made). The probability of both of these events occurring, while at the same time about three thousand different protein molecules are simultaneously being produced by chance out of some sea of amino acids, with the enzymatic effect appropriate to promote replication of DNA, metabolism, production of RNA, creation of cell walls, etc, is zero three and four times over. One could go on and on with this line of reasoning, but the point is made.

The evolutionist/atheist will cry that given sufficient time, this could happen. That is simply not true. Time will not increase the probability. Even the building block molecules needed to synthesize these huge molecules would not last very long at all. For example, consider a quote from Melvin Calvin, the Nobel Prize winner, from his book *Chemical Evolution*:

> I should like to discuss the stabilities of these classes of molecular "fossils." There are two important classes of materials that I have not yet mentioned, namely amino acids coming from the peptides, and carbohydrates coming from various kinds of polysaccharides. I have not described the amino acids or carbohydrates of the mud because both of these compounds may be expected to, and do, disappear quite rapidly. They do not remain as stable compounds for very long periods of time in any large amounts.[4]

Calvin is discussing studies of chemicals found in the decomposed mud below lakes. He notes, as any chemist could have predicted, that the building blocks required to produce life, in this case amino acids and polysaccharides (sugars), are very short-lived.

[4] Melvin Calvin, *Chemical Evolution* (Oregon State System of Higher Education, Eugene, Oregon), p. 34.

He could have said the same about the building blocks of nucleic acids as well. The fact is that even these compounds, much simpler than proteins, still have fairly low entropy, and, with time, decompose to more stable molecules. These molecules simply do not last. Although the right mix of chemicals with some energy added, such as that described by Urey and Miller, could produce a low level of some of the amino acids, it could be predicted that these compounds will decompose fairly rapidly to simpler molecules rather than continuously build up over time. Simply allowing for "sufficient time" would never allow the concentrations of these compounds to build up to any appreciable level.

As an analogy, imagine a film of a large building being blown up, as is done sometimes in the present day to old buildings. The viewer would see entropy increasing at a very rapid rate! Now, imagine that film running backwards. One would be seeing entropy dramatically decrease. In other words, it is an impossible process. A random pile of twisted rubble made up of iron, concrete, pieces of broken glass, plastic, styrofoam, wood, and so forth would never spontaneously be turned into a building. Time would not increase the probability at all. In fact, it would actually decrease the likelihood of a building forming spontaneously, because presumably the first rain storm would scatter the stuff even more widely. Similarly, life could not have formed spontaneously, and time would not increase the probability of this happening.

To sum up this part of the argument, the known laws of nature simply do not allow for life to "just happen." No amount of jumping up and down will change this fact. Covering up this fact with a lot of scientific jargon does not change the reality either. The concept of "chemical evolution" with molecules gradually getting more and more complex due to natural selection flies in the face of laws that chemists know and use every day. The huge and incredibly-complex molecules required for a living thing to function are not, never have been, and never will be produced spontaneously. If not even one of these molecules could be produced, then surely the precise proportion of several thousand different molecules of this type could never be produced simultaneously and in the same place. See the appendix for a further, more technical discussion of the relationship between the second law of thermodynamics and the origin of life.

Belief in the production of life by some sort of spontaneous process requires a level of faith which far surpasses the faith required to believe in the inspiration of the Bible, or to believe in the resurrection of Jesus Christ from the dead. The inspiration of the Bible and the resurrection of Christ should "not be accepted without proof" either, but at least both claims have a great deal of evidence to support them. The level of faith required to believe in the spontaneous generation of life makes atheism in essence a form of religion. One might reasonably ask the scientist: "Do you really believe this happened?"

Why would a trained scientist believe the claims of Carl Sagan, Melvin Calvin and the others about how life began? Why do Sagan and Calvin and others believe in these ideas themselves? The answer is that they assume that there is a natural explanation for everything. They are convinced that God does not exist. They "know" there is a scientific explanation for everything, including the origin of life. To quote Hearn and Hendry:

> This does not mean that scientists will necessarily ever be able to create life, although this certainly seems within the range of scientific possibility; it does mean, however, that *reputable scientists* do *have faith that life arose from inanimate matter* through a series of physico-chemical processes no different from those we can observe today.[5] (emphasis mine)

Here a scientist who believes in this theory is admitting that this amounts to a kind of faith. This statement about atheism is true. It requires great faith to believe in atheism. On the other hand, I personally do not agree with Hearn and Hendry that all reputable scientists agree with this theory that life "came about by a long series of singularly beneficial accidents." I would like to think of myself as a reputable scientist, and I definitely do not agree that life came about by a "natural" process.

Why would anyone prefer to put their faith in science rather than the God who created him or her in the first place? Let the atheist answer the question for themselves, but consider a quote from Romans 1:18-20:

> The wrath of God is being revealed from heaven

---

[5] Walter Hearn and Richard Henry, *Evolution and Christian Thought Today* (Paternoster, London, 1959), p. 67.

against all the godlessness and wickedness of men who suppress the truth by their wickedness, since what may be known about God is plain to them, because God has made it plain to them. For, since the creation of the world God's invisible qualities—his eternal power and divine nature—have been clearly seen, being understood from what has been made, so that men are without excuse.

According to the Bible, the existence of God is obvious from the observation of nature, of the universe, and of God's greatest creation: man. A scientist who looks at the unimaginable complexity and beauty of the universe, of nature, or of the molecules which make up life has been provided with more than enough reason to believe in God.

A question may arise at this point, "what about the evidence for evolution?" The creation of life and evolution of that life once it is created are separate scientific questions. The evidence for the theory of evolution and a discussion of how it relates to the Biblical account is discussed in chapter eight. Bear in mind for now that if God created one life form, it certainly seems reasonable that he might equally as well have created a number of different species at different times. It will be shown that the evidence from the fossil record is consistent with this view.

We will now turn our discussion from a refutation of scientific atheism to questions relating to science and the Bible.

FOR TODAY

1. In your own words, what does the second law of thermodynamics say about the creation of life?

2. What is the significance of the four classes of biological molecules to the argument against the spontaneous generation of life?

3. You were given a somewhat complicated argument for why protein creation requires nucleic acids and vice versa. Could you explain that argument to someone else?

4. How do you believe life came about? Why do you believe what you believe?

5. What does the nature of living things say about the nature of the creator of life?

But avoid foolish controversies and genealogies and arguments and quarrels about the law, because these are unprofitable and useless.

Titus 3:9

5

WHAT ABOUT GENESIS?

It is time to change gears dramatically. In chapters three and four, it was shown that atheism does not stand up to scrutiny when the laws of nature are used in an attempt to explain the existence of the universe or the existence of life. The existence of the universe and of life both require a creator. The evidence explored so far does not reveal all that much about the nature of the God who created all these things. Which "God" created the universe? Which "God" created life? Was it Allah (the Muslim God)? Was it Brahman (the chief of the Hindu gods)? Was it the God of the Bible? Maybe it was some still-unknown God who has chosen not to reveal himself to mankind.

Science is certainly not one of the main themes in the Bible. However, the Bible does contain information and claims of a scientific nature. Careful analysis of the parts of the Bible which relate to things scientists talk about will provide dramatic evidence that the Creator of the universe has revealed himself in this great book. It is probably true that science does not provide the most convincing proof of the inspiration of the Bible. One could look at internal consistency, fulfilled prophecy or historical accuracy, among a great number of other areas, which provide great evidence for the inspiration of the Bible. The interested reader should investigate these topics, which happen to be outside the range of discussion in this book. While other areas might provide even more dramatic support for the Bible than that from science, a careful and thoughtful investigation of how science relates to the Bible will provide further strong support for belief in its divine authorship.

First, consider the statement of someone who could represent the atheist view in regard to the relationship between science and the Bible. To take as a typical statement, a quote from the well-known atheist Delos B. McKown:

> Christianity is scientifically unsupported and probably insupportable, philosophically suspect at best and disreputable at worst, and historically fraudulent.[1]

This claim, a fair summary of the point of view of most atheists and humanists, is easy to make, but does this claim stand up to an open-minded, reasoned analysis of the scripture? This question will be examined carefully.

Lest it be said that all well-known modern scientists are anti-God, a quote from the most famous scientist of our century, Albert Einstein would be worth considering.

> Science without religion is lame, religion without science is blind.

He explains himself by saying:

> Science can only ascertain what is, but not what should be, and outside its domain, value judgements of all kinds remain necessary.[2]

Einstein believed that science, in and of itself bereft of moral truth, is lame without religion as a source of moral truth and as a guide to the purpose of man.

Atheists typically assume that there is a rational explanation for everything that ever has or ever will occur in the universe. To quote from another humanist:

---

[1] Delos B. McKown of Auburn University, an essay in *Science and Religion* (Greenhaven Press, San Diego, California, 1988), pp. 65-71.

[2] Albert Einstein, *Out of My Later Years*, (Citadel Press, Secaucus, New Jersey, 1955).

Science, on the other hand, assumes that there are no transcendent, immaterial forces, and that all forces which do exist within the universe behave in an ultimately objective and random fashion...A non-mysterious understandable universe is a basic assumption behind all science.[3]

Personally, I wish this author would speak for himself. Not all scientists assume there is absolutely no transcendent, immaterial force at work in the universe. A strong argument has already been made that it is necessary to be very careful about what assumptions are made in approaching such a question. In fact, it has been shown in this book that scientific knowledge available concerning the nature of the universe and of life prove beyond a reasonable doubt that a "transcendent force" does indeed exist. If the basic assumption of the humanist/atheist is false, then isn't it likely that their conclusions will fall apart as well? Do not be deceived. This so-called basic assumption of science is just that, an assumption, and a false one at that!

Those who would attack the Bible often begin by confidently pointing out the Genesis "myth" as proof of the ignorance of the writers of the Bible. It could be conceded that whoever wrote the account in the first chapter of Genesis was not a trained scientist. However, as will be shown here, despite the scientific "ignorance" of its writer, the Genesis story itself is not at all scientifically ignorant. In fact, the scientific insight of the creation story of Genesis, coming from a writer who was not privy to our modern-day scientific knowledge provides further proof of divine authorship of the Bible. The goal, then, is to look closely at this most controversial book.

Since in this section the first chapter of Genesis will be discussed in some detail, it would be helpful if the reader would pull out a Bible and read this chapter. Consider as a starting point a rough outline of the creation account. It might go something like this:

1. God existed before the creation of the universe.

2. God created the universe out of nothing.

---

[3] Norman F. Hall, Lucia K. B. Hall, "Is the War Between Science and Religion Over?" an article in *The Humanist*, May/June, 1982.

3. After creating the universe and everything in it, God created life.

4. Last of all, God created man.

Before beginning to look at the specifics of Genesis chapter one in more detail, consider this bare-bones outline first. Is there anything here in conflict with the known facts of science? Does Genesis one mess up on the order of things? In fact, doesn't Genesis offer a more reasonable explanation of how the universe got here "out of nothing" than the atheist? The atheist can describe the big bang, but cannot explain how or why it happened. The big bang theory has the universe appearing out of nothing, in agreement with the Genesis account. The problem with the big bang theory is that it cannot explain what caused the explosion which initiated the universe. There is strong evidence that the big bang occurred, but who or what caused it to "bang"? Is there any scientific precedent for massive amounts of matter suddenly appearing out of nothing? As stated before, conclusive proof that the big bang actually happened will prove elusive, but it just so happens that the biblical account could explain how and why it happened.

What about how life came to be? The Bible claims here in Genesis that all life was created by God. Despite their claims, it has been shown that scientists simply cannot provide a believable scientific explanation of how life just came to be by some accident of nature. Atheists may not be willing to admit it, but the existence of life on the earth is truly a miracle. God takes credit for this miracle in Genesis.

In addition one finds here in Genesis the claim that man came last of all of God's creations. Again, the Bible has it right on. Fossil evidence shows man, the highest of all creatures, to be one of the most recent species to appear on the earth.

Let it be pointed out that this is not a scientific explanation. The creation of the universe and the creation of life have no scientific explanation. Why? They were miraculous events. In the final analysis, the existence of life is a miracle. It has been revealed in the discussion previously that the closer one looks at the unimaginable complexity of even the simplest life forms, the stronger the case for miraculous creation becomes. In addition, the more physicists explore the possible origins of the universe, the more strongly the evidence requires a miraculous explanation for its beginnings. The interesting fact is that the Bible just happens to get it right, despite the fact that the writers had little if any scientific training or knowledge to draw on as they wrote. First God, then the universe, then life, then man.

Now take a closer look at the details of Genesis chapter one. To quote a few phrases from the first five verses. "In the beginning, God created the heavens and the earth... And God said, "Let there be light," and there was light... And there was evening, and there was morning—the first day." For the sake of simplicity, three possible approaches to understanding the Genesis account will be described and discussed.[4] One could:

1. Take the entire Genesis account in its literal, face-value sense, including six twenty-four-hour days of creation. This would imply that the earth is very young.

2. Take the entire account as an outline from God of what he did in creating the earth, but assume that the six "days" are not literal, but rather a simplification made for the sake of scientifically unsophisticated readers.

3. Completely discount the entire Genesis creation story as having any validity at all. One could take it to be just another of a number of similar creation "myths" which were a common feature of ancient cultures—a nice piece of poetry.

To the person who knows very little about the Bible, the third approach makes perfect sense. In a secular/humanistic culture for which science has become a virtual alternative religion, why consider a book over two thousand years old as a source of truth? However, to the person who realizes that science cannot explain how we came to

---

[4] A number of other approaches to explaining and interpreting the creation account in Genesis have been proposed. In general these are either relatively similar to one of the three explained in this chapter or of little importance in the opinion of the author. For a concise but reasonably comprehensive description of various explanations see Alan Hayward, *Creation and Evolution* (Bethany House Publishers, Minneapolis Minnesota, 1995).

be here, this approach may not be sufficient.

Many people cannot help but ask the three big questions: "How did I get here?," "Why am I here?," and "Where am I going?" Humans have an innate sense within themselves that there must be a purpose to life—a meaning to this whole thing. If science cannot explain the origin of man, perhaps the creator might have revealed himself in some other way. Inevitably, someone searching for the truth will end up considering the Bible. There, the open-minded person will find undeniable marks of inspiration.

To the person who recognizes the Bible "...as it actually is, the word of God" (1 Thessalonians 2:13), choice #3 above is not an option (hopefully this would not be an untested assumption, but rather a conclusion derived at least in part from the evidence). For this person, the Bible is not a collection of fables, myths and other nice stories. Nevertheless, it would be helpful for this person to challenge themselves to at least temporarily consider the possibility of the Bible containing errors, for if they assume the answer before doing the investigation, it is easy to predict what the result will be. If nothing else, skeptical friends will not be able to respect this type of approach if they catch on that this is what is happening. Some of them may very well be able to see through an intellectually dishonest approach to the truth. For those who would tend to fall into category #3, please be challenged to at least consider the other two views in the light of scientific knowledge. When one decides to take the Genesis account seriously, one finds a surprising correlation with scientific fact.

THE "LITERAL" INTERPRETATION OF GENESIS CHAPTER ONE

Let us consider the first alternative described above: the face-value interpretation of Genesis chapter one. There are two points worth making right up front about the literal twenty-four hour understanding of the book of Genesis. First, this would be the most obvious interpretation of the chapter. If one simply read the account for itself, without looking through the lens of modern-day science— "And there was evening, and there was morning-the first day."—the most obvious way to interpret these words would be to assume that each of these events occurred in one twenty-four-hour period.

This, however, leads to the second point about this view of

Genesis. The fact is that the earth appears to be billions of years old. Despite the attempts of the creationists to fabricate an alternate view, the earth appears to be old. It is not necessary to review the evidence discussed previously, but the evidence could be summarized by stating that there is an apparent conflict between the face-value, literal interpretation of Genesis chapter one and scientific fact.

So how can the literal interpretation of the creation account be reconciled with the facts of science? First of all, it has already been shown beyond a reasonable doubt that the universe was created. Besides that, life was created. Could an all-powerful God create the world in six twenty-four-hour days? The answer is obviously, yes. Scientific evidence supports the creation of life. The question is simply how and when was life created. The cosmos was created. The remaining issue is the means and timing of that creation. To the person who is convinced that the Bible is inspired, and that the God of the Bible is all-powerful, the creation account in the first chapter of Genesis is quite believable.

When Jesus created enough bread and fish to feed five thousand people, the bread and fish were created with an "appearance of age" (John 6:1-13). In fact, the fish was cooked already. It would be difficult to speculate how "hard" it is for God to do these sorts of things, but one thing one can be confident of is that the universe exists, and it was created by God.

It should be noted, however, that the literal interpretation of Genesis is not a scientific theory. By definition, a scientific theory concerns known or measurable physical facts, which are governed by predictable natural laws. A miraculous event clearly is a violation of these natural laws. The law of conservation of mass was violated when Jesus made fish out of nothing that day by the sea of Galilee! This "theory" that God created the world in six twenty-four hour periods, even if it is true, is not something to be taught in science classes. It could be mentioned off-hand as a possible starting point for how the universe eventually came to be what it is today, but even if it is true, it seems reasonable to believe that it would not be verifiable by any scientific experiment. Although science can be used to support the concept of creation, it cannot by its nature be used to prove a particular miracle occurred.

Some who claim to be Christians are very defensive about this point, but they should not be. Those committed to thinking through this issue carefully should not be intimidated by creationists into accepting the untenable position that scientific evidence supports an age of the earth of only a few thousand years. The literal understanding of Genesis chapter one is not scientific by any definition of science. Being based on a miraculous event, it cannot be disproved by science, but it is not scientific. It would be a belief based primarily on faith in the Bible.

For those who take the Genesis creation account at face value, let the author play "devil's advocate" briefly in order to challenge their thinking. First, if the earth is only a few thousand years old, how can the fossil record, containing such apparently ancient species as dinosaurs and trilobites buried under hundreds or even thousands of feet of younger-appearing sediment, be explained? One could turn to the flood theory, but that theory appears to be discredited. The fact is that if the earth is only a few thousand years old, then dinosaurs never lived. Bogus claims of dinosaur tracks appearing together with supposed human footprints not withstanding, if the earth is only a few thousand years old, then triceratops, pterodactyls and a host of other species found only as ancient fossils never lived. This is a strong claim, but it seems impossible to reconcile the fossil and sedimentary evidence with both a few thousand year-old earth and the existence of some of these seemingly extremely ancient species.

Besides, what about very distant galaxies, hundreds of millions or even billions of light years away from us? How has the light from a galaxy five million light years away from us managed to reach us if the universe itself is only seven thousand years old? If the universe were only a few thousand years old, then we should only be seeing objects a few thousand light years away, and new objects should appear to pop into existence when the light created since they were formed finally arrives here to be seen by us.

There are a multitude of similar questions that could be asked along these lines, a few of which were raised in the second chapter, but two will suffice to make the point. How will the person who takes Genesis chapter one at face value answer these questions? More to the point, how will they answer these questions without resorting to the false claims of creationists?

These are good and challenging questions, but there is a reasonable answer. They might reply by claiming that when God created the world, he created it with an appearance of age. When the earth was formed, it included fossils already imbedded in the ground. Also, at the moment when God created the stars, he also created light on a path from the stars to the earth, just exactly as if they had already been there for a very long time.

Playing "devil's advocate" just a little bit more, people who take Genesis chapter one literally could ask themselves why God would put fossils of animals which never even lived in the ground? If the earth actually is young, why would God have made it appear old? It would almost be as if God were trying to test people's faith, or as some critics would say, it is as if God were deceiving us. In answer, the believer might reply, "It is clear from nature that God created the world as it is. Who am I to tell God how to create the world? God, in His wisdom, could create the world in any way he wants. God revealed in Genesis chapter one how he created the world, and I believe it."

In summary, the believer who takes the literal interpretation of Genesis relies on faith in the inerrancy of the Bible rather than scientific evidence as the basis for his belief. Through the fulfilled prophecy from the Old Testament, through the undeniable power of the words of Jesus, through the historically confirmed resurrection of the Lord Jesus Christ, and many other powerful proofs, this person is convinced that the Bible is the inspired word of God. It is no huge leap of faith for the believer to conclude the account in Genesis is no less accurate than all the other accounts in the Bible. It so happens that there is no scientific evidence available to disprove the literal interpretation of the creation account in Genesis as an accurate record of the miraculous means by which God created the world we live on and the life it supports. It seems only fair that those who would take a different view (for example the "non-literal" approach described below) respect the intellectual and spiritual right of others to interpret the Genesis creation account in this way.

THE "NON-LITERAL" INTERPRETATION OF GENESIS CHAPTER ONE

Next, the second approach described above for understanding the Biblical account of creation will be considered.[5] To quote from

---

[5] A well written description of some alternative views of Genesis which provides some alternative views of Genesis to those provided here, with a stronger theological perspective is found in a book by Douglas Jacoby, *The God Who Dared* (Discipleship Publications International, Woburn, Massachussets, 1997, www.dpibooks.com)

above, one could "Take the entire account as an outline from God, of what He did in creating the earth, but assume that the six 'days' are not literal, but rather a simplification for the sake of scientifically unsophisticated readers." According to this view, the Genesis creation account is God's way of explaining to his people how he created the world. Neither the level of scientific knowledge nor the vocabulary of the Hebrew language would allow God to reveal the concepts of genetics, geology, chemistry or physics necessary to fully explain what he did when he created the world.

In the next two chapters, a number of astoundingly accurate scientific insights will be described which were revealed by God in the Bible to these scientifically unsophisticated Hebrews. The creation account is no exception to this rule. In each case, when God revealed to his people some truth with scientific implications, he did not choose to give a detailed scientific explanation, but rather used terms accessible to readers of the day.

In order to bring out this point, consider the creation account in more detail. Assume for the moment that the account is given from the point of view of an observer on the earth (Genesis 1:1). This "observer" would first note that the sun, as it was formed, began to produce light. As the earth formed, it would be spinning, and there would be periods of light and darkness (Genesis 1:3). Later, as the earth "evolved," a separate atmosphere and ocean formed (Genesis 1:6-8). Next, as the planet cooled, lighter rock such as quartz and granite rose above the heavier basalt; high enough to appear above the surface of the oceans, creating the first continents (Genesis 1:9,10). God created the first life forms (Genesis 1:11-13), gymnosperms (non-fruit bearing) before angiosperms (fruit bearing). As the plants proliferated, they absorbed large amounts of carbon dioxide from the atmosphere, allowing the earth to cool enough that the thick clouds finally parted, allowing an observer on the surface of the earth to see the sun and the moon for the first time (Genesis 1:15-19). Next, God created many different species of the higher life forms such as birds, reptiles and mammals. (Genesis 1:20-25). Last of all, God brought to fruition, his highest creation, man, *homo sapiens*. (Genesis 1:26-28).

It seems reasonable to ask where all the supposed scientific blunders are in this description. The Genesis "myth," as some would call it, does not seem to reflect the lack of knowledge of its authors, but rather shows an uncanny insight into scientific truth. Allowing for the simplification in language God used in order to communicate with a people of no great sophistication, the first chapter of Genesis just happens to agree in outline form with modern scientific knowledge. The Bible believer is not surprised at this fact, but the skeptic should take note.

To put the account of creation in Genesis into context, it will be helpful to briefly describe current scientific theories of the history of the solar system and life on the earth. The evolutionary theory of the origin of the solar system would predict that the sun and its planets formed from a cloud of interstellar matter as it condensed due to gravitational attraction. According to the second law of thermodynamics, when gases contract, they increase in temperature. As the gas cloud, which eventually formed our solar system contracted, the innermost matter reached sufficiently high temperature and pressure to initiate fusion of hydrogen, and the gas cloud became a star. As the disk-shaped cloud contracted rather than falling into the sun, the matter farther from the center was spinning around the sun fast enough that it coalesced to form planets.

Initially, the planets had fairly thick atmospheres made up of mostly hydrogen and helium, with perhaps smaller amounts of methane, water and so forth, but the innermost planets lost a significant amount of their atmospheres due to their light weight and the intense solar wind. Because on the inner planets the lighter elements were lost in this way, there existed a higher proportion of the heavier elements. As these inner planets cooled, an outer crust of solid rock formed. On the earth, the proper temperature and sufficient quantity of water allowed the formation of a layer of water to cover the entire planet. As the crust cooled, the lighter rocks were pushed upward, forming the continents. As the proper conditions existed to support life, living forms appeared. First very simple one-celled species appeared. Eventually, simple organisms capable of photosynthesizing appeared which reduced the carbon dioxide in the atmosphere, but raised the amount of oxygen to significant levels, probably for the first time. This created the proper conditions for animals which use oxygen to appear. As time progressed, ever more complex and adapted species were seen on the earth.

The account above is a fusion of theory as well as scientific evidence. It just so happens that there is an incredible correlation between the account in Genesis and this model. Should one be surprised at this?

It would be interesting at this point to compare the biblical account of creation to those from cultures and religions of antiquity. For example, Greek myth includes the claim that all the animals were originally formed by Prometheus and Epimethius from clay molds, analogous to the production of cast iron. Greek myth also involves the idea that Atlas holds the sky up above the earth on his shoulders, as well as the dubious claim that the sun rides in a chariot across the sky each day.

Ancient Egyptian religion included a belief about creation as well. It involved the belief that in the beginning the universe was filled with a primordial ocean called the Nun. The waters of the Nun were stagnant. Out of the limitless flood rose the primeval hill, which eventually became the landmass of the earth. The priests of each of the great cult centers of Egypt claimed that their city was the point where the landmass of the earth originated. Some believe the great pyramids at Giza represent this primeval hill.

The Babylonian creation myth involved gods emerging from a divine swamp which had existed forever. These gods came out of the swamp in male and female pairs. As the younger gods appeared, they did battle with the older gods. In one battle, Marduk, the son of Ea (the earth God) attacked and killed the first god of all, Tiamat. He caught her in a net and crushed her skull. As the divine blood of Tiamat spilled to earth, the Babylonian creation myth claims that the blood and mud mixture formed the first humans.

The ancient and traditional religion of Japan is Shinto. Shinto scripture holds that two gods Izanagi and Izanami were given a gift of a spear adorned with jewels. At the time of this gift, the earth was a muddy chaos over which the gods had flung a bridge. Izanagi and Izanami went out on the celestial bridge and thrust their spear into the muddy chaos. They drew it back all spattered with mud. A little fell off the spear, falling to earth, forming one of the Japanese islands. Then these two gods came and lived on this island. Out of their union the eight principal islands of Japan were created.

It would be difficult to say with authority what the Hindu creation story is as there are a great number of different and sometimes even contradictory lists of gods and myths about those gods depending on what period of Hinduism is being considered. One myth has the first man Manu arriving on an earth devoid of animals. Out of a sacrifice Manu offers to the gods, the first woman was made. Manu lusted after the woman, so she changed into a cow. Manu changed himself into a bull, and from their offspring cattle were created. Next, the woman changed into a goat, and Manu changed himself into a he-goat and so forth until all the animals were created.

A creation myth of the Iroquois nation relates that in the beginning of things there were two brothers, Enigorio and Enigohahetgea. The former went around the world furnishing it with gentle streams, fertile plains and good fruits. The latter followed him maliciously creating rapids, thorns and deserts. Eventually Enigorio turned on his brother, crushing him into the earth, where he still lives, receiving the souls of the dead and existing as the author of evil.[6]

It would be possible to quote from creation accounts from the Popul Vuh, the ancient Mayan scripture, or from the creation stories of other Native Americans, from Buddhist scripture and so forth, but these examples are typical. These creation accounts make for an interesting study, but it would be very difficult to take them seriously from a scientific point of view. The Bible is a striking exception to this rule. Scholars and theologians may want to put the biblical account of creation into the same basket as these creation myths, but it seems to be a good idea to ask whether or not this is good scholarship. Here, then, is very strong evidence, not that the Bible contains a bunch of myths and legends, but rather that the Bible is inspired by God.

The well-trained skeptic would point out the other creation account in Genesis chapter two. Everyone knows that this second account is a separate myth, in total conflict with the first myth in Genesis chapter one—or so would the atheist or even some theologians claim. Perhaps some believers have not heard this one yet! It is a fairly common criticism of intellectuals who do not believe in the Bible. They claim that the initial editors of Genesis had a debate over which account to include, finally deciding to put both creation stories in despite their "contradictions." This is easy enough to claim, and it gives theologians some nice topics for their Ph.D. theses, but the relevant question to be asked is whether or not it is true.

In fact, Genesis chapter two is not an account of the creation of the world at all. It is an account of the creation of Adam and Eve. A careful study of the second chapter of Genesis will show that it is an account of the creation and fall of man. "And God formed man from

---

[6] Daniel G. Brinton, *The Myths of the New World*, reprint of the 3rd edn., (Genealogical Publishing Company, Baltimore Maryland, 1974), p. 79.

the dust of the ground" (Genesis 2:7). It represents a relatively small proportion of what is described in Genesis chapter one as having occurred on the sixth day. Where is the contradiction between the general creation account in the first chapter and the specific description of part of the sixth day in the second chapter of Genesis?

It is time for the author to play the part of the "devil's advocate" in order to challenge the thinking of the person who would take the view of the Biblical account of creation just described. To do this, the literalist would ask: "Why do you choose not to take what God said at face value? God said 'there was evening, and there was morning— the first day'. Where is your precedent for simply assuming that God did not mean exactly what he said?" This is a good question. As pointed out above, the most obvious interpretation of the first chapter of Genesis would be to assume that God is describing literal twenty-four hour days. In fact, if one were to be completely honest, they would have to admit that if it were not for knowledge gleaned from science, completely apart from the Bible, they would probably not even have considered any other way of thinking about the creation story in the Bible.[7]

The intellectually honest person must answer this question. A general rule of Biblical interpretation, or of interpretation of any writing for that matter, is that the obvious interpretation is generally the correct one. Unless there is a definite reason from the context or from information elsewhere in the writing to support another interpretation, the "obvious" interpretation should be taken as the original meaning. In this case, it certainly would seem that the obvious way of understanding Genesis chapter one would be to assume that it is speaking of creation in six twenty-four-hour days, not billions of years. How would the person who believes the "non-literal" interpretation of Genesis respond to this question?

This person might respond as follows. First, they might claim that God did not intend to give a step-by-step, detailed account of creation. It was not God's intent to include a great amount of detail of relevance to science. In fact, what God wanted to communicate was that he was the creator of the universe, of all life, and finally of man.

---

[7] This statement is actually not entirely true. There are a number of examples of both Jewish and Christian intellectuals in the pre-scientific age who held to some sort of a non-literal interpretation of Genesis chapter one. These people did not have access to scientific knowledge, yet held that the non-literal approach was most reasonable.

God is the all powerful creator, to whom we must give account. If God had told the Hebrews that he first created prokaryotic life, without a definite nucleus in the cell, followed by eukaryotic life, with a separate nucleus in the cells, he probably would have lost his audience right then and there since they did not even know what a cell was. God chose to give a very simple account of what he did, in the order he did it.

Secondly, to answer the "devil's advocate," this person might look a bit closer at the Hebrew language used in the Genesis account. Here, the word for "day" is the Hebrew word *yom*. In fact, this is the same word contained in the name of the Jewish holiday Yom Kippur, the Day of Atonement. What does this word mean? In the King James Version of the Bible of 1611, the word *yom* is translated as follows:

> 1181 times as "day" (but with several different connotations
> of the word)
> 67 times as "time"
> 30 times as "today"
> 18 times as "forever"
> 10 times as "continuously"
> 6 times as "age"
> 4 times as "life"
> 2 times as "perpetually"

Clearly, this word has many possible meanings, depending on the context. Even when it is translated as day, the word does not necessarily refer to a twenty-four hour period. For example, to quote Isaiah 4:2, "in that day the Branch of the Lord will be beautiful and glorious, and the fruit of the land will be the pride and glory of the survivors in Israel." Here, even though the translators used the word "day," in translating the word *yom*, the context does not seem to imply a literal twenty-four hour period, but rather an indefinite period of time. It was not hard for the translators of the Bible to decide to use the English word "day" in the context of Genesis chapter one for the Hebrew word *yom*, but it would be a mistake to be dogmatic about the interpretation of the passage as implying literal twenty-four hour periods.[8]

---

[8] A novel and interesting approach to thinking about the six days of creation can be found in a recently published book by Gerald L. Schroeder, *The Science of God* (Broadway Books, New York, 1997). Schroeder uses the concept of relativistic

Another question, which could be asked, is whether the events described in the creation account as occurring in six "days" could actually happen in twenty-four hour periods. A look at the sixth day of creation as described briefly in chapter one and in more detail in chapter two shows that in this day, God created a number of kinds of animals first, followed by Adam. On this day, Adam named all the creatures in the garden. Despite the novelty of all this, Adam had time to get very lonely. He fell asleep, and while he was sleeping, Eve was created. It seems hard to believe all this could have happened in a literal twenty-four hour day.

In summary, the Bible believer might conclude that Genesis chapter one is an outline account of what God did over a great span of time as he created the universe. Looking more closely at the text, they would discover that this account just happens to square with currently available scientific evidence about the history of the earth.

THE THIRD APPROACH TO GENESIS CHAPTER ONE

What about the third approach to understanding Genesis chapter one? One could "completely discount the entire Genesis creation story as having any validity at all." It could be treated as just one of many interesting man-made myths; essentially the same as a number of other creation stories common to most ancient cultures. As has already been said, for the person who knows little or nothing about the Bible, this would seem at first glance to be a perfectly reasonable conclusion. It would seem to be reasonable unless one begins to look more closely at the accuracy of the Genesis account.

This third approach does not conflict with current scientific knowledge. In fact, the statement above contains no testable scientific claim. Nevertheless there are some questions which people who hold to this view should ask themselves. First, how can the agreement of the Biblical account of creation with scientific knowledge be explained? This question should be especially challenging in the light of the creation myths created by other peoples as described above because these other creation stories certainly do not jibe with current scientific understanding at all.

---

time dilation to produce a mathematical model which contains the fifteen billion year history of the universe in six literal days. A Ph.D. physicist and a theologian, Schroeder combines mathematical rigor, careful theology and some speculation to produce a theory which the reader may find worthwhile wading through.

Second, when one considers the weight of the evidence for the inspiration of the Bible, does it seem wise to simply assume that the Genesis creation account is just a myth created by scientifically ignorant people? The person who is prepared to "blow the whole thing off as a myth" may not have looked carefully at the evidence for the inspiration of the Bible. They would be well advised to read the Bible carefully, first of all, and to follow up this careful reading by considering such topics as the resurrection of Christ and Biblical prophecies about the Messiah.

Speaking for myself, if I had never read the Bible and seen it working in my life, if I had never studied the Old Testament prophecies (which predict in amazing detail the birth, life, betrayal, death and resurrection of Jesus Christ), if I had never looked into the truth of the resurrection of Christ, I might have reached the same conclusion about the creation story in the Bible. In view of the marks of inspiration which pervade the Bible, and which distinguish it from the writings of all other world religions, it becomes very difficult for a reasonable person to dismiss the book of Genesis as a myth. When the scientific accuracy of the Biblical account of creation is compared to the fairy-tale creation stories of ancient cultures, one cannot help but be impressed with the Bible—the Word of God.

Bringing together the descriptions of the three possible approaches to the creation account in Genesis, it seems reasonable to ask at this point which one should be believed. Should Genesis chapter one be interpreted as implying literal twenty-four hour periods or not? The readers must decide for themselves. The answer "I don't know" is always an option. From the tone of this chapter, the reader could probably surmise that the author leans toward the non-literal view, rather than the literal twenty-four hour interpretation of Genesis chapter one. But that is just one person's opinion. It is the opinion of someone who is a scientist and who is prone to being impressed with scientific evidence.

The fact is that one could never absolutely prove how or when the universe was created. It is impossible to go back into the past and do an experiment to determine what happened. The fact is that creation did occur. There is consistent evidence that it occurred a very long time ago. However, the possibility remains open that God could have created the universe with an appearance of age.

It seems reasonable to ask whether one's personal interpretation of the first chapter of Genesis is an issue of major importance or not.

Creationists often make the point that acceptance of the literal interpretation of Genesis is essential to faith in Jesus Christ. Some creationist writings seem to imply salvation hangs on whether one accepts the six twenty-four-hour day creation doctrine or not. A careful reading of the New Testament will not support this view. In Luke 13:3 Jesus said "But unless you repent, you too will all perish." As far as is known, Jesus never said "But unless you accept that the world was created in six days, you will all likewise perish." The six-day doctrine is not even mentioned in the New Testament. If this issue was an important one, it could be assumed that God would have somehow made it clear.

It makes sense to assert that any question which does not affect a person's salvation or their daily relationship with God could safely be dismissed as not a major issue. To quote from Titus 3:9, "But avoid foolish controversies and genealogies and arguments and quarrels about the law, because these are unprofitable and useless." Christians would be well advised to carefully consider the issue of creation. However, it would seem that heated, drawn out debates about the "correct" interpretation of the Biblical creation account would fall into the category of "unprofitable and useless" controversy.

The creation account is not the only example of scientific knowledge dramatically supporting belief in the inspiration of the Bible. In the next two chapters several examples of the Bible being in dramatic agreement with scientific evidence will be described, offering further reason to believe in its divine authorship.

FOR TODAY

1. What was your belief/opinion about Genesis chapter one before reading this book?

2. Have your beliefs in this area changed at all from what you have read? How and why?

3. This chapter leaves the final answer of interpreting Genesis 1 to the reader. How do you feel about having an important

question for which you cannot determine the truth absolutely?

4. Do you believe it is a significant matter to the Christian faith whether Genesis chapter one was intended to be taken literally or not?

5. Specifically, what would you say in answer to Delos McKown's claim that "Christianity is scientifically unsupported and probably insupportable?"

6. Do you believe dinosaurs, trilobites and so forth actually lived at some time? How does this belief relate to your understanding of the Genesis creation account?

RECOMMENDATION

Find a book about creation "myths" and check out the claim in this book that the Genesis account stands alone amongst these stories.

*If you listen carefully to the voice of
the Lord your God and do what is
right in his eyes, if you pay attention
to his commands and keep all his
decrees, I will not bring on you any
of the diseases I brought on the
Egyptians, for I am the Lord who
heals you.*

Exodus 15:26

6

RATTLESNAKE FAT, ANYONE?

It is a commonly held belief that the Bible, especially the Old
Testament, is a collection of myths and fables, dreamed up by a
number of rabbis to justify their own conception of God. The truth of
this sort of claim is not difficult to test. If the Bible contains the
musings and imaginings of a number of religious men separated in
time by hundreds of years, then it would be expected to contain
inconsistencies of message, obvious historical exaggerations and
mistakes. More relevant to the subject addressed in this book, it
would also contain references to scientifically related issues which
would reflect the almost complete lack of scientific knowledge of its
writers. The Bible would contain many "old wive's tales." Its concept
of things such as the origin of the earth, medical knowledge, geology
and world geography would be a reflection of the myths and folk
beliefs of the Egyptian, Babylonian, and other cultures which
surrounded the Israelite nation.

A look at other writings more or less contemporary to the writers
of the Old Testament reflects the description above. For example,
consider Herodotus, the greatest of the ancient Greek historians (484-

425BC), considered the father of the study of history. Although he was a great thinker, innovator, and collector of historical information, his histories mix truth with legend, and are tainted by ethnic prejudice. Most of the histories left behind by the ancient cultures of the day (notice how the word day can be used to mean something other than a twenty-four hour period) were commissioned by a king or other government official as a record of their accomplishments. These records invariably show a blatant prejudice, extolling the virtues of the current regime, minimizing or ignoring its defeats and faults.

However, there is one historical record of the time which is in total contrast to this pattern—the Bible. In the Bible, one finds a record uniformly consistent with known facts about rulers and cultures of the region at the time in which the accounts are set. Perhaps even more startling, the Bible records the defeats, mistakes, and sins of the leaders of the nations of Judah and Israel. It does so in lurid detail. The greatest king in the history of Israel is David, the slayer of Goliath. He was the general who united the nation and defeated the Philistines, the Arameans and all the enemies of Israel. He is described as a man after God's own heart, the greatest poet and songwriter of the people of God. Yet in the Bible one also sees his failure as a husband and a father. He is seen to fall into lust, adultery and even murder. No book of its time can even come close to the Bible in both accuracy and honesty as history.

But what about science and the Bible? The Bible, especially the Old Testament, because it is a record of how God dealt with his people, contains a great deal of information of a historical nature. On the other hand, references to issues of scientific relevance are relatively scarce in the Bible. Nevertheless, to the extent that the Bible does contain claims or references of a scientific nature, it provides further dramatic proof of the inspiration of the Bible.

Of the different fields of science, it is the area of medical knowledge that the Bible touches on the most. There are such a large number of Biblical references to medical science issues that this entire chapter will deal exclusively with this topic. In the next chapter areas of science other than medical knowledge which are touched on in the Bible, will be investigated.

The first five books of the Old Testament were often referred to as "the Law" by the Jews. For example, when Jesus said in Luke 24:44 "Everything must be fulfilled that is written about me in the

Law of Moses, the Prophets and the Psalms," he was referring to the three divisions in the Hebrew Bible. These three divisions are the Law (*Torah* in Hebrew, Genesis-Deuteronomy), the prophets (*Nevi'im* in Hebrew, Joshua-Esther except Chronicles as well as Jeremiah-Malachi) and the Psalms (or "Writings," *Kethubim* in Hebrew, Job-Song of Songs, Chronicles). The third book of the Law is Leviticus. This book contains the largest portion of legal code in the Old Testament. A number of regulations can be found in Leviticus which are related to health and diet issues. These examples will now be examined closely

Before doing this, however, it will be useful to consider the nature of medical knowledge in cultures immediately surrounding Israel in the time frame of the writing of Leviticus. If the Bible is simply a book written by man, its allusions to medical questions would reflect the level of insight or ignorance of the dominant cultures in the Near East at the time in which it was written. On the other hand, if the Bible is inspired by God, one would expect it to show insight which reflects that inspiration.

Of the ancient cultures surrounding Israel, the Egyptians are considered by many to have been the most advanced in medical knowledge. Through trial and error, their books perhaps contain some useful knowledge. However, some of the prescriptions in them would not stand up to modern science, to say the least. A quote from the famous Embers Papyrus, a medical text written about 1550 BC, prescribes "To prevent the hair from turning gray, anoint it with the blood of a black calf which has been boiled in oil, or with the fat of a rattlesnake" or concerning hair-loss, "When it falls out, one remedy is to apply a mixture of six fats, namely those of the horse, the hippopotamus, the crocodile, the cat, the snake, and the ibex.[1] Other prescriptions from the Embers Papyrus include such drugs as dust-of-a-statue, shell-of-a-beetle, head-of-the-electric eel, guts-of-the-goose, tail-of-a-mouse, fat-of-the-hippopotamus, hair-of-a-cat, eyes-of-a-pig, toes-of-a-dog, and semen-of-a-man.[2] These medicines seem humorous to the modern reader, but the consequences of this medical and scientific ignorance was surely devastating to the people of that day. These examples are brought up not so much to reveal the ignorance of the Egyptians at that time, but to provide a background

---

[1] S. E. Massengill, *A Sketch of Medicine and Pharmacy* (S. E. Massengill Co., Bristol Tennessee, 1943), p. 16.

[2] C. P. Bryan, *The Papyrus Embers*, (D. Appleton, New York, 1931).

against which one may compare the writings of the Old Testament:
writings from approximately the same time period as those of the
Embers Papyrus. In looking at Old Testament health laws, the author
would acknowledge significant contributions in this area from a book
by S. I McMillen, MD.[3]

Throughout history, the Jewish nation as a whole has been noted
for its medical knowledge. At least part of the reason for this fact can
be discovered from a look at some Bible passages which gave the
Jews an advantage in medical science. To the extent that they
followed the "prescriptions" in the Old Testament, the Jews were
automatically way ahead of their time. However, to show how
advanced in areas of medicine the Israelites were in and of
themselves, apart from the revelation of the Old Testament, consider
an excerpt from a Jewish book of medical knowledge from a time
roughly contemporary to the writing of the New Testament.[4]

> "Whatever God created has value." Even the animals
> and the insects that seem useless and noxious at first sight
> have a vocation to fulfil. The snail trailing a moist streak
> after it as it crawls, and so using up its vitality serves as a
> remedy for boils. The sting of a hornet is healed by the
> housefly, crushed and applied to the wound. The gnat,
> feeble creature, taking in food but never secreting it, is a
> specific against the poison of a viper, and this venomous
> reptile itself cures eruptions, while the lizard is the antidote
> to the scorpion.

Would anyone like to try any of these prescriptions? Also, note
the scientific error regarding the digestive system of gnats. It seems
reasonable to agree with the writer that "everything God created has
value," but most people would presumably not be eager to try out
these prescriptions. This passage is typical of the writings of the Jews
of the age as well as those of the Egyptians and other cultures at the
time. However, it is in remarkable contrast to what can be found in
the Bible, as will be shown. Why? Because the Old Testament writers
were lucky? Because the scribes were using the scientific method to

---

[3] S. I. McMillen, M.D., *None of these Diseases* (Power Books, Old Tappan,
New Jersey, 1984).

[4] Lewis Ginsberg, *The Legends of the Jews*, (Jewish Publication Society of
America, Philadelphia, 1956), p. 23.

carefully examine their medical practices? Or could it be a sign that the Bible is no ordinary book, but rather the inspired Word of God. As the following sections are presented, the readers should judge for themselves.

Please note that no one is claiming that all the medical knowledge of the ancients, be they Egyptian, Chinese, Indian, Greek, Native American, or any other is mere superstition. Through trial and error methods, some of the most ancient cultures evolved medical folklore which is of some value. However, this folklore inevitably contains a large proportion of remedies which are about as effective as using rattlesnake fat to prevent premature grayness.

As mentioned before, this study will focus primarily on the book of Leviticus, the book of Law received by Moses from God at a time contemporary to the writing of the Embers Papyrus. Moses himself was born in Egypt in more or less the same time period as the writing of the Embers Papyrus. Anyone who would claim that the Bible is just the record of the opinion of the Hebrew nation of the day should consider comparison of Leviticus to the Embers Papyrus.

To begin, consider a remarkable claim made by God through Moses to the nation of Israel while they were wandering in the wilderness for forty years, as recorded in Exodus 15:26.

> If you listen carefully to the voice of the Lord your God and do what is right in his eyes, if you pay attention to his commands and keep all his decrees, I will not bring on you any of the diseases I brought on the Egyptians, for I am the Lord who heals you.

Here God is claiming that if the nation of Israel will obey his decrees, they will avoid all kinds of diseases. History bears out the ramifications of this claim. The Jews have always been a relatively small nation, yet they have survived repeated invasions and even attempts at extermination. Time and again the Assyrians, the Babylonians, the Greeks and the Romans as well as others have attacked and scattered the Hebrew people. Although scattered, the Jews have somehow always managed to recover and to grow in number. One factor in the resilience of the Jews was their health practices as inspired by the Old Testament.

For example, consider Leviticus chapter eleven. A summary of this section is given here, rather than a detailed quote. In this chapter, God tells his people that pigs, rabbits, rodents, crustaceans, lizards, and all carnivores are "unclean"—in other words not acceptable to be eaten. On the other hand, the fish with scales, cows, sheep, goats, and certain non-carnivorous birds are "clean." It just so happens that all the animals on the unclean list are relatively dangerous to eat unless very thoroughly cooked. Pork is the type of meat which is most famous for being considered "unclean" by the Jews. Pork is also famous for causing trichinosis. On the other hand, beef, fish and lamb are relatively safe. All of these types of meat, if handled properly, may be eaten safely even when uncooked (although certain safety precautions are highly recommended). Is this coincidence?

How did Moses know which types of meat were relatively safe? Did he learn it from the Egyptians? Certainly not, for they often ate many of the unclean meats, especially pork. Did he run some controlled scientific experiments? That seems very unlikely. The nation of Israel at the time was relatively ignorant scientifically, but the Law contained in the Bible reflects a different level of knowledge. It is not at all unreasonable to think that the ultimate author of the Law, God, was protecting his people from "the diseases I brought on the Egyptians."

Next, consider Leviticus chapters 13 and 14. Here one finds very specific laws regarding several different types of infectious skin diseases, including leprosy. Specific instructions are given to quarantine the subjects with certain skin diseases for a set period of time, to burn their clothing and even destroy the pottery implements off of which they had eaten.

Throughout time, the spread of leprosy has been blamed on such causes as heredity, the eating of certain foods, or even on the alignment of the planets. These false ideas naturally led to an inability to stop the spread of the disease. Finally, after thousands of years of human suffering, leprosy was finally brought under control in the Western world in the Middle Ages.

> Leadership was taken by the church, as the physicians had nothing to offer. The church took as its guiding principle the concept of contagion as embodied in the Old Testament....This idea and its practical consequences are defined with great clarity in the book of Leviticus....Once the condition of leprosy was established, the patient was to be segregated and excluded from the community. Following the precepts laid down in Leviticus the church undertook

the task of combatting leprosy...it accomplished the first great feat...in methodical eradication of disease.[5]

The incredible devastation which has been caused by leprosy throughout Europe, Africa and Asia could have been largely avoided if the medical practitioners had simply heeded the command in Leviticus 13:46. "As long as he has the infection he remains unclean. He must live alone; he must live outside the camp." In fact, once quarantine was initiated, leprosy was dramatically reduced. Does anyone believe Moses made this up because he was a brilliant doctor, or because of the great medical knowledge he had acquired in Egypt? Even if someone was a skeptic who believed that the book of Leviticus was written by a group of Jewish priests at around 500 BC rather than by Moses at around 1400 BC, how could they explain the discovery of quarantine by these priests over two thousand years before its general application in Europe?

In 1873, Dr. Armauer Hansen identified the bacterium which causes leprosy, proving once and for all that it is indeed an infectious disease (medical science refers to leprosy as Hansen's disease). Today, if caught early, it is entirely curable.

Three years later, the Norwegian Leprosy Act was passed. This law ordered lepers to live in precautionary isolation away from their families. In 1856, there were 2858 lepers living in Norway. By the turn of the century, only 577 lepers were left; and that number plummeted to 69. By 1930 the spectacular discoveries of science allowed Norway to control this disease, but the precautions had been written down by Moses almost 3,500 years earlier.[6]

Fortunately, leprosy can now be controlled by antibiotics, so that there is no longer a need to quarantine lepers. However in the time of the writing of the Old Testament, God's prescription was the most effective way to prevent the spread of this disease.

Next, consider another law contained in the Bible in Numbers chapter 19. It would be useful to read that chapter before continuing. Here one finds the command from God that anyone who touches the

---

[5] George Rosen, *History of Public Health* (MD Publications, New York, 1958), pp. 62-63.

[6] S. I. McMillen, M.D., *None of These Diseases*, Power Books, 1984, p. 22.

body of a dead person is to be considered unclean for seven days. In addition, they are to be considered unclean until several very precisely specified hand and body washings have been completed. Even the person who aided in the cleansing was required to wash himself.

God specifically prescribes the use of water containing ash and hyssop. The ashes in combination with the oil of the hyssop plant made a kind of soap. It just so happens that the hyssop plant, a type of marjoram which grows in the Middle East, contains in its oil about 50% carvacrol, an organic compound almost identical to the commonly used antifungal and antibacterial compound thymol. Therefore, ash and hyssop work both as a soap and as a natural antibiotic. Does it seem reasonable to believe this was just luck on Moses' part?

It is extremely interesting to note that the stringent practice of hand washing between the touching of patients or after touching dead bodies was only introduced to "modern" medicine by the work of Ignaz Semmelweis in the 1840's and 1850's. Semmelweis worked at that time in a hospital in Vienna in which one in six of the maternity patients died in the hospital. No wonder women preferred to have their children at home! These depressing statistics were typical numbers for hospitals at that time. Semmelweis noted that a typical practice for the doctors in hospitals was to perform autopsies on the patients who had died the previous day before immediately proceeding to examine their patients. Today, of course, one cringes to hear of this practice, but it should be noted that the concept of infectious disease was not introduced to the world or proved by modern science until the nineteenth century by the work of the likes of Pasteur, Lister and Semmelweis. Semmelweis ordered that all doctors performing autopsies must wash their hands thoroughly before working with live patients. There was an immediate fourteen-fold decrease in mortality. If only doctors had heeded the commands of Moses concerning washing after the touching of dead bodies before this date!

Semmelweis eventually noted that even touching of a maternity patient after touching another live patient could result in infection, so he further ordered hand cleansing between obstetrical examinations. The mortality rate went down further. Semmelweis could have referred to Leviticus chapter 12 at this point where women who give birth are proclaimed to be "unclean" for seven days. It is now known, of course, that the nature of childbirth, which opens the circulatory system of the mother to outside infection makes it a particularly dangerous practice for doctors to move from one maternity patient to another without a very thorough washing. This remains true for several days after childbirth. The Bible prescribes seven days. Fortunately, thanks to modern science, obstetricians do not need to wait seven days between examinations. Nevertheless one can see that if medical practitioners had obeyed the practice described in the Law of Moses, millions of unnecessary deaths could have been prevented.

It is an interesting side note that the work of Semmelweis was not easily accepted by the medical establishment, to say the least. He was ridiculed by many of his peers in the medical community. Eventually, he was persecuted so strongly that he was fired from the hospital where he did his original work. Even after publishing convincing proof of the effectiveness of hand washing, he was scorned by his peers. Eventually, Semmelweis was committed to a mental institution where, ironically, he died of a blood infection.

Semmelweis was not the only proponent of germ theory to be persecuted. Louis Pasteur, the great French chemist, proposed the existence of viruses to explain such infectious diseases as smallpox and rabies. Despite the successes in curing diseases such as smallpox, his virus theory was vigorously opposed. One of his opponents, Guerin, even challenged him to a duel.

But there is more! For example, consider Leviticus 17:13,14.

> Any Israelite or any alien living among you who hunts any animal or bird that may be eaten must drain out the blood and cover it with earth, because the life of every creature is its blood. That is why I have said to the Israelites, "You must not eat the blood of any creature, because the life of every creature is its blood; anyone who eats it must be cut off."

Quite apart from the obvious health dangers in eating blood unless it is very thoroughly cooked, one finds an interesting statement here. "The life of every creature is its blood." The function of blood in carrying life-giving oxygen as well as all the other nutrients to the cells of the body was not discovered until the past century. Indeed, "bad blood" was one of the chief (incorrect) diagnoses of medical science for all kinds of symptoms until the nineteenth century. The red and white stripes of the barber's pole represents a common practice of barbers in the Middle Ages as well as right up to the nineteenth century: bloodletting! When someone had an infection or some other medical problem, a very common treatment was to attach leeches to suck out the bad blood from the patient. A study of the record of the treatment leading up to the death of George Washington shows an unusually large number of bloodletting's, prompting some to suggest that he may have actually died primarily from a loss of blood.

The fact is that the blood is the carrier of "white blood cells," the body's chief means of protection against all kinds of disease. Bloodletting never helped anyone to get well. If only medical practitioners had taken the opportunity to read the Bible on this subject: "The life of every creature is in its blood." God was trying to protect his people so that they would not be overcome by "any of the diseases I brought on the Egyptians" (Exodus 15:26).

Consider circumcision. This practice was actually instituted a few hundred years before the time of Moses, during the lifetime of Abraham. In Genesis 17:12 one can read:

> For the generations to come every male among you who is eight days old must be circumcised, including those born in your household or bought with money from a foreigner—those who are not your offspring.

There are two points to be made here. First, is the command to circumcise all males. Second is the command to circumcise all these males on the eighth day. Circumcision is a painful process! Why would God have had his people go through this? From a theological point of view, God established circumcision as a mark of the covenant he was making with his people. It just so happens that there are interesting medical implications to this command as well.

Consider circumcision itself. Whether to circumcise or not is a matter of some debate even among the scientific community today. Because of the level of daily hygiene, the need for this somewhat radical procedure has been reduced dramatically in the United States. However, in a culture such as that of Israel over three thousand years ago, personal hygiene was certainly not up to the level available to most people today. In Old Testament times, people went extended periods without bathing. The warm, damp area behind the male foreskin is an excellent breeding ground for all kinds of bacteria and fungi. In our culture, with a much greater opportunity to care for hygiene, this does not present nearly so great a danger for the spread of disease. Consider, however, the advantage to God's people in this practice, both for preventing the spread of sexually transmitted diseases, as well as for preventing any of a number of common infections. God could have commanded his people to take a bath every day, but this would have been impractical, especially as they wandered in the desert for forty years.

There is another medical advantage to circumcision. In 1932, Dr. A. L. Wolbarst of New York reviewed the records of 1,103 cases of cancer of the penis.[7] Not one of these cases was a Jewish patient. Considering the proportion of Jewish men in New York, the fact that none of the cancer patients was Jewish was an astounding revelation. In fact, cancer of the penis is virtually unknown among Jewish men. Up until 1975, only six cases of this disease among Jews were recorded.[8]

Perhaps there is some sort of genetic resistance to this type of cancer among Jews. Three large studies have shown that of 521 cases of cancer of the penis, none of the subjects had been circumcised.[9] Considering that roughly half the male population of the risk-group was circumcised, this provides a statistically convincing case for the efficacy of circumcision in preventing this horrible, often fatal disease, whether or not one is of a Jewish background. There is also a considerable literature in addition to the studies mentioned. Those interested should refer to the book by Dr. McMillen mentioned above for a more thorough treatment of this subject. While circumcision is not a 100% sure preventative, it apparently virtually eliminates the threat of cancer of the penis. Those who make emotional arguments in opposition to the circumcision of males would do well to pay attention to the admonition of the book of Genesis.

Did God institute circumcision of males for these health reasons, or did he have in mind only the theological implications? That would be hard to say since it is never specifically referred to in the Bible as beneficial to health. Whatever the case, there is clearly a pattern developing here. When the Jews followed the commands of the

---

[7] A. L. Wolbarst, *Circumcision and Penile Cancer*, Lancet, 1, (1932), 150-153.

[8] E. Leiter and A.M. Lefkovits, "Circumcision and the Penile Carcinoma," *New York State Journal of Medicine*, 75, (1975), 1520.

[9] C.W. McMillan, A. E. Weis and A. M. Johnson, "Acquired Coagulation Disorders in Children," *Pediatric Clinics of North America*, 19(1972), 1034.

Bible, they were protected from all kinds of diseases. Could this be just coincidence? Or is the Bible the inspired Word of God?

It is interesting to note that circumcision is much safer if performed on infants. In our modern culture, when older boys are circumcised, typically due to inability to retract the foreskin, the operation requires either general anesthesia, with its attendant risk of death, or a local anesthetic, which has been known to cause permanent impotence. On the other hand, circumcision of an infant is a simple and safe procedure. Within the first three weeks of birth, circumcision causes pain, of course, but the symptoms disappear immediately after surgery. On the other hand, adults experience pain for at least a week.

This leads to the next point. Why circumcision on the eighth day? While circumcision of a male child on the second or third day in a hospital setting is virtually completely safe, for the Israelites this was not necessarily the case. It has been noted by pediatricians that the risk of hemorrhage for children increases dramatically from about the second to the sixth or seventh day of life. After this point, the risk drops dramatically. Again, in a hospital, under proper care, circumcision between the second and seventh day of life is quite unlikely to lead to major permanent harm: but in the conditions of surgery prevalent in the times of the Old Testament, the implications are significant.

The reasons for this effect are now well known. Upon birth, the level of vitamin K in a baby is similar to that of its mother. However, the body does not produce its own supply of this nutrient, necessary to the production of the protein compounds used by the body to cause blood clotting. Instead, bacteria present in the intestines supply vitamin K to the body. Infants are born without the required bacteria in their intestines. It takes a few days for the bacteria to build up to the point that a safe level of vitamin K is reestablished. This level is reached by about the eighth day. Today, because of the research on vitamin K levels, doctors give shots of this important vitamin to newborns. Without these shots, the most preferred day for performing a safe and relatively less painful circumcision is somewhere between the eighth to tenth day of life, according to medical science. In fact, one of the clotting proteins produced through the agency of vitamin K, prothrombin, actually peaks out at approximately 110% of its normal level on about the eighth day.

Abraham clearly did not have access to these data, nor any way to generate it. Why did he tell the people of Israel to circumcise on the eighth day? Or even if someone was a dyed-in-the-wool skeptic who will not even admit that Abraham ever existed, how could they explain that this is in the Bible? Presumably, the skeptic would claim that it is just luck or coincidence. How many coincidences will need to be pointed out before some are convinced that this book is inspired by the same God who created life in the first place?

As another example (if another is needed), one can find in Leviticus 18 laws against incest. Specifically, the Jews were commanded not to marry or to have sexual relationships with blood relations. This would include aunts, uncles, and cousins. Incest was a common practice of the day, continuing right up to modern times. Again, God may have had reasons of his own, but it just so happens that children born from a union between close blood relatives have shown a much higher incidence of genetic disease. Moses did not say why to avoid this type of behavior, but for the Jews who followed these decrees, much disease and heartache was avoided.

A brief trip through the Bible will reveal an almost innumerable list of commands which lead to our emotional as well as physical well being. For example, one discovers in Leviticus 7:22-25:

> Do not eat any of the fat of cattle, sheep or goats....Anyone who eats the fat of an animal from which an offering by fire may be made to the Lord must be cut off from his people.

It would be interesting to think about how much lower the rate of arteriosclerosis and death due to heart disease was among the Israelites who obeyed this decree. The discovery of the direct correlation between animal fat consumption and death due to coronary heart disease is a recent one, but God provided protection to his people from this, the greatest killer in the western world.

In Proverbs 23:20 is written "Do not join those who drink too much wine or gorge themselves on meat." Both admonitions are good health advice, as has been well documented. Note that the Bible does not forbid consumption of either meat or wine in moderation. Meat in moderation can be an important part of a healthy diet. It would seem that the medical jury is still out on whether wine in moderation is harmful, or possibly even beneficial to health, but clearly much wine is extremely injurious to both mental and physical health.

Most of the commands above are unique to the Bible, providing an overwhelming weight of evidence of its inspiration. God's commandments concerning sexual relationships, although not unique to the Bible, provide still more evidence of the wisdom and practical nature of this great book in bringing health and happiness to anyone who will follow it. God specifically forbids homosexuality (1 Corinthians 6:9,10, Leviticus 18:22 and Romans 1:26,27), prostitution (1 Corinthians 6:9,10), adultery (Proverbs 5), and indeed any kind of sex outside of marriage (Galatians 5:19).

There is a pervasive belief in our "modern" society that open attitudes about sexual lifestyles is a good thing. The media plays down the significant minority in America who still accept the Biblical teaching that sex outside of marriage is wrong. The prevailing attitude in our culture is that sexual experience before marriage, preferably with more than one partner, is a good thing— leading ultimately to greater sexual fulfillment. History, however, will prove that the opinion of the majority does not equal truth. Trust is an essential key to a healthy marriage relationship. There is a huge benefit to be reaped for those with enough self-control to delay sexual gratification until a commitment to a lifelong relationship has been sealed. If only people would listen to God's commands in this area! The emotional benefits (let alone the spiritual benefits) to human lives would be incalculable.

Obedience to the Biblical teaching in this area would yield benefits to our physical well being as well as to our emotional health. Sexual promiscuity is certainly nothing new. Homosexual and heterosexual prostitution was at the heart of a great number of ancient religions. The list of sexually transmitted diseases, including gonorrhea, syphilis, hepatitis and AIDS seems to be always growing. These diseases would be wiped out in short order if people only had the wisdom and self control to obey God's will. The amount of death and destruction wrought by a refusal to follow God's commands is difficult to comprehend.

In conclusion, God was not playing the part of a cosmic politician—promising much but delivering little—when he promised Israel that if they would obey his commands he would not bring on them any of the diseases of the surrounding peoples. However, God's principal interest was not in the physical health of his people. He was much more interested in their spiritual well being. For a person who is willing to consider the Bible as their spiritual PDR (physician's desk reference), God has left many marks of inspiration, not the least of which are the commandments relevant to medical science.

FOR TODAY

1. Do you believe the health-related commands which were given to Israel were primarily intended to protect the people's health, or do you believe God gave the commands for other reasons, and they just happened to be good for the Hebrew nation's health?

2. Can you think of any laws in the Old Testament which would have been bad for the Israelite's health?

3. We made a little fun of the rattlesnake fat cure for premature grayness. Can you think of any modern-day health claims, which have proven to be more or less equivalent to using rattlesnake fat?

4. Can you think of any reasonable argument to refute the claim that God's plan for circumcision on the eighth day provides evidence for the inspiration of the Bible? Try to do this, even if you are inclined to believe the argument.

RECOMMENDATION

Prepare a list of health-related commands in the Old Testament. Next, divide the list into those which would still be in force under the New Testament, and those which would no longer be laws for Christians. Finally, ask yourself which of the Old Testament commands would still give us health benefits, even with our modern medical technology. Do you see a pattern?

Always be prepared to give an answer to everyone who asks you to give the reason for the hope that you have.

1 Peter 3:15

7

FABLE OR FACT?

Although the greatest number of references in the Bible relevant to science are related to medicine, there are also a number of references in the Bible of interest to geologists, biologists, astrophysicists and others. These will be considered in this chapter.

It has already been shown that the scientific sophistication of other cultures contemporary to the Hebrews was primitive to say the least. The picture from Greek mythology of Atlas holding up the sky, while interesting to contemplate, cannot be taken seriously as being "scientific." Such myths were prevalent even among the Greeks, considered almost universally to be the most advanced of ancient cultures in scientific learning. This backdrop of relative scientific ignorance is the environment in which both the New and Old Testaments were written.

Just in case someone might be under the illusion that the Jews were ahead of their contemporaries in science learning, giving a possible explanation for some of the scientific insight in the Bible, consider a quote from a Jewish writer of roughly the same historical period as that of the New Testament.[1]

The flood was produced by a union of the male waters,

---

[1] Lewis Ginsberg, *The legends of the Jews*, (Jewish Publication Society of America, Philadelphia, 1956), p. 76.

which are above the firmament, and the female waters issuing from the earth. The upper waters rushed through the space left when God removed two stars out of the constellation Pleiades. Afterward, to put a stop to the flood, God had to transfer two stars from the constellation of the Bear to the constellation of the Pleiades. That is why the Bear runs after the Pleiades. She wants her children back, but they will be restored to her only in the future world.

Male and female waters? Water flowing out of a constellation? Hmmm.... This passage, representing the bias and scientific errors of the Jews of Jesus' day, serves as an example of the kind of material which surely would have crept into the Bible if it were written according the wisdom of the Jews at the time. It is simply impossible to find a passage of similar nature to this one anywhere in the Bible. Let the skeptic be challenged to find an exception to this claim. Miracles are recorded in the Bible, but they are presented as miracles. Myths and fables with obvious scientific mistakes such as the one quoted above are completely absent from the Bible. This is a big claim, but it is either true or it is not. The reader who finds it hard to accept should simply check it out for themselves.

Consider for example a passage in the Old Testament which might be of interest to a biologist. In Genesis 16:4 one can read concerning Abraham that "He slept with Hagar and she conceived." Probably for the majority of Bible readers, this scripture and the scientific implications would slip right on by. Here the Bible is claiming that conception occurred in Hagar after sexual relationship with Abraham. A possible response would be "no kidding," but it just so happens that it was not proven until the nineteenth century that conception occurs in this manner. It is an interesting exercise to look at old medical textbooks from the eighteenth century replete with neat diagrams showing how men deposited the already conceived baby into the nice warm female nursery. In the Qur'an, the scripture of Islam, one can read that man deposits the baby in the womb (Sura 16:4, Sura 22:5, Sura 23:14). Because the Q'uran was written by man, it reflects the knowledge of man. The Bible gets it right again.

What about cosmology? In Job 26:7 it is stated that "He spreads out the northern skies over empty space; he suspends the earth over nothing." This is an amazing statement. Here one finds the Bible proclaiming that the earth is freely moving in space, not attached to anything else. Simple observation of physical events in the world would cause one to believe that everything falls down. Not surprisingly, using simple human reasoning, the ancients either pictured the earth as a flat plate-like object resting on some larger object or as being the literal center of the universe, with the sun, moon, planets and stars attracted to the earth and circling it once a day. This second idea, called geocentrism, was the dominant theory of intellectuals up until the modern era. Popular religion generally held to ideas like the first. However, the biblical book of Job gets it right.[2] The earth is suspended on nothing. In fact, it moves through the universe under the influence of the force of gravity, primarily from the sun. That is quite an insight for a scientifically ignorant people!

Did anyone else come up with this idea in so ancient a time? There is no record of this idea being proposed as early as this. Actually, a few hundred years after the writing of Job, some Greek astronomers, Anaxagorus and Democritus among them, did reach this conclusion. However, the great mass of people as well as the supposedly wise men throughout history have held to ideas such as that contained in the Sutras, part of the scripture of the Hindu religion. Here we find the statement that the earth is on the back of four elephants on top of a turtle, encircled by a serpent, swimming in a sea of milk. Are the Sutras inspired by God? What about the Vedas or Upanishads, other Hindu scriptures? These questions deserve thought, but it should be noted that each of these contain stories as scientifically suspect as the elephant/turtle/milk story.

Another common misconception of the ancients was that the sky is basically like a bowl, with all the celestial objects moving at the same distance from the earth across the circumference of this bowl. The scriptures of the Jain religion (a religion native to India) go a bit further to describe different levels of the heavens, with different celestial objects revolving at different distances from the earth. Obviously, none of these ideas bear any resemblance to the facts about the universe. The reason is that they are of human origin.

Concerning the stars, one can read in Jeremiah 33:22 "I will

---

[2] In analyzing Job 26:7, the reader should bear in mind other passages in the book such as Job 9:6, in which an earthquake is metaphorically described as God making the earth's "pillars tremble." Job is a book of poetry, written in a dramatic style. It is not a systematic treatise on cosmology. Nevertheless, Job 26:7 is in striking agreement with our present knowledge of cosmology.

make the descendants of David...as countless as the stars of the sky..." Here the Bible is stating that the stars cannot be counted. Again, this may seem like an obvious point, but the number of stars in the sky was the subject of debate in the Near East in Jeremiah's time (about 550 BC). Greek philosophers speculated and debated about the total number of stars. Democritus, one of the Greek philosophers, is the first person known to have proposed that the Milky Way is actually unresolved stars, and that therefore there are an inconceivable number of stars in the universe. Actually he was the second, counting Jeremiah.

About the earth itself, one can read in the Bible in Isaiah 40:22 that the earth is round (the Hebrew word can also be translated "sphere"). Most who thought about such things at the time of the writing of Isaiah (about 750 BC), believed the earth was flat. In about 525 BC, the Greek mathematician Pythagoras (famous for the Pythagorean theorem) was the first person known to have claimed that the earth is a sphere. The first, that is, if one is to ignore Isaiah! In about 150 BC, Erastosthenes, a Greek living in Alexandria, measured the circumference of the earth indirectly. He was accurate to within about ten percent.[3]

By the way, to clear up a common misconception, although the uneducated people of Columbus' day may have believed in a flat earth, the majority of intellectuals in the fifteenth century believed, along with Pythagoras and Erastosthenes, that the earth was spherical. Columbus did not have to convince Queen Isabella that the earth was round—he just had to convince her the voyage was a good financial investment. However, Isaiah, writing two thousand years before Columbus was ahead of his time. Is it unreasonable to conclude that his writing was inspired by God? In fact it seems fair to ask if it is reasonable to think that it was *not* inspired.

The point is not so much that Isaiah beat Pythagoras, but that the Bible, to the extent that it reflects scientific knowledge, appears to get it right every time. By contrast, consider the Qur'an: written in the twenty years or so before the death of Mohammed in the year 632 AD. Mohammed claimed to be a prophet of God. If the claim is true,

---

[3] Author's note. It may be a mistake to make too big of a deal out of Isaiah 40:22, since the Hebrew word has an ambiguous meaning, and the point of Isaiah is spiritual, not scientific. Nevertheless, the Bible does not have anything equivalent to the turtle/elephant/milk story. In any case, whether round or spherical, Isaiah gets it right.

then the Qur'an would be accurate to the extent that it can be compared to scientific knowledge. In the Qur'an it is written that the sun and stars revolve around the earth (Sura 21:33). This would be in agreement with the Greek concept of the universe prevalent in Mohammed's time, called the geocentric theory. The only problem is that it is wrong. The reason the sun and stars appear to circle the earth is that the earth is spinning on its axis. This should cause one to question the scientific accuracy of the Muslim scripture.

But there is more. For example, the Qur'an records a piece of the sky falling and killing someone (Sura 34:9, Sura 52:44). In Sura 15:18 it is stated that shooting stars provide protection from evil spirits. In Sura 12, one can read about the eleven planets. In Sura 18:9-19 is contained a story of a group of boys who fell asleep in a cave with their dog. They woke up three hundred years later and left the cave. This would just be a quaint fantasy if it weren't for the fact that it is recorded as if it were a true story in the scripture of one of the world's major religions. The Q'uran has king David making an iron coat of mail (Sura 34:11) before such a thing was ever invented. There are other examples which could be given, but the point is that the Bible does not contain these kinds of mistakes.

To the ancients, rain itself was a mystery. Where does the rain come from? Why is it that the rivers continually flow into the sea but the sea does not ever overflow? It would be interesting to explore some of the fables and myths produced by ancient cultures to explain this phenomenon. The Greeks invoked the gods to explain the phenomenon. In Amos 5:8, it is stated that it is God "who calls for the waters of the sea and pours them out over the face of the land." Also, in Job 36:27 is found the statement that God "draws up the drops of water, which distill as rain to the streams." In other words, the Bible describes a cycle which begins with water evaporating from the surface of the earth, condensing, and distilling back to the earth, only to evaporate and return to the earth again. The correct explanation of this process, called the hydrological cycle, gained general acceptance by the scientific community only in the previous century. The Bible has it right again, three thousand years before man, on his own power, was able to answer the question. Skeptics would claim that the Bible is a book written by scientifically ignorant people in a scientifically ignorant age. To their surprise, the Bible gets it right again.

Another example worth mentioning is found in Genesis chapter six. Here God describes to Noah the dimensions of the ark. The ark is to be 300 cubits long by fifty cubits wide by thirty cubits high. It just so happens that the thirty to five to three ratio of length to width to height for the construction of large ships has been found, both from long experience of oceangoing nations and from engineering principles to be the ideal dimensions for a balance of large volume, stability and speed in the building of great ships of commerce. It is not clear that the ark needed to be built for speed, but large volume and stability were definitely important issues. Historically, the Hebrew nation has never been an oceangoing people. This was especially true in the early part of their history. Up until the time of Moses, the Jews were primarily a semi-nomadic tribe. How, then, did the writer of Genesis get the ideal dimensions for a large ship right? Could it be that God had a hand in providing this knowledge?

Some who would attack the Bible have tried to find passages which reveal its scientific errors—similar to those quoted above from the scriptures of other major world religions. The examples which have been used have either been events which are clearly claimed by the Bible itself as miracles, or they have been quotations from clearly poetical passages. As an example of the former, skeptics have referred to the parting of the Red Sea as an example of biblical scientific "mistakes." There certainly is no natural explanation for the Red Sea spontaneously parting (despite efforts of some to find one). However, this event is unquestionably described as a supernatural miracle, not a natural event. The Bible writers never attempt to portray the parting of the Red Sea as being the result of a natural phenomenon. The parting of the Read Sea is only a "mistake" if one assumes that miracles have never occurred.

As an example of a supposed biblical scientific error which is simply a misinterpreted poetical passage, consider Isaiah 11:6-9. In this scripture, it is written that "the wolf will lie down with the lamb, the leopard will lie down with the goat" and "The infant will play near the hole of the cobra." This is a poetic and prophetic reference to the future kingdom of God. In God's kingdom, all kinds of people who would never have come together because of deep-rooted class, ethnic or nationalistic hatred will join hands in God's family. It is not a prediction that cobras will suddenly make good pets. The claim that Isaiah 11:6-9 is a scientific blunder shows a lack of understanding of the context and meaning of the scripture.

In what might come across as desperation, some have used 1

Kings 7:23 in an attempt to show that the Bible contains scientific blunders. Here the diameter of a circular bowl in the temple is given as ten cubits, while its circumference is quoted as thirty cubits. Using a more exact value for the number "pi," the author of 1st Kings could have said the circumference was 31.415 cubits, but apparently he rounded off a bit. It seems unreasonable to use the biblical author's rounded off dimension as evidence of a scientific mistake, to say the least.

As has been stated, many people believe that the Bible, and especially the Old Testament, is a collection of fables and the imaginative musings of a scientifically ignorant people. In response to this claim, one could ask; which fables? Where are all these examples? When the writings of the Bible are compared to a few brief examples from ancient Jewish writers as well as from the scriptures of other religions, one finds a contrast so striking as to be unexplainable. Unexplainable, that is, unless one allows for the possibility of the inspiration of the Bible.

This book, which the skeptic would claim is the product of ignorance, is laced with accurate claims of a scientific nature, which should cause any open-minded person to question the validity of the atheistic/humanistic attacks on the Bible. Go ahead, be skeptical. Good idea. Do not assume anything to be true unless the evidence speaks for itself. If a person will with a sincere heart and an open mind make a decision to study out the Bible, they will eventually have "accepted it not as the word of men, but as it actually is, the word of God, which is at work in you who believe." (1 Thessalonians 2:13) Not only that, but if a believer is willing to be intellectually honest enough to question what they believe about the scientific accuracy of the Bible, they will have even greater convictions which will allow their faith to weather the storms of life.

FOR TODAY

1. Read Psalm 74:12-14. Would this represent a scientific "blunder" in the Bible? Why or why not?* What about Jonah 1:17 and 2:10?*

2. Play devil's advocate for a moment. How might you attempt to defend, for example, the Hindu account of the turtle and the milk etc.? What about the Qur'an's mentioning of eleven planets?

RECOMMENDATION

Locate a copy of the Qur'an. Find the suras referred to in the text of this chapter. Apply the same sort of standards you used in question #1 above to see if the claim in this book that these are scientific blunders is true.

* Author's answer: In the first case, Psalm 74 is a poem. The writer is using poetic license to make a point about God, not to present a scientific argument that some sort of sea monster exists. In the second case, what happened to Jonah is clearly presented as a miraculous event.

Could anyone survive in the belly of a huge fish for an extended period of time? I would have to say no. That is why what God did for Jonah is such a great miracle. A miracle, by the way, which Jesus said prefigured his three days in the tomb (Matthew 12:40), an event which science certainly cannot explain.

*It is mere rubbish thinking at
present of the origin of life. One
might as well think of the origin of
matter.*

Charles Darwin

8

WHERE DID I COME FROM?

There are a few good questions one could raise regarding the relationship between science and the Bible which have not yet been addressed. For reasons which will become apparent presently, some of these questions have been left for the later chapters of the book. Three of these questions will be discussed:

1. What about evolution?
2. What about Adam and Eve/the origin of man?
3. What about the flood?

All these questions have been referred to in at least a passing way in the body of the book, but they deserve more attention. The first two, being closely related, are covered in this chapter, while the third is covered in chapter nine.

EVOLUTION

No question related to science and the Bible has generated more controversy and even outright animosity between creationists and atheists than the question of evolution and the related question of the origin of man. Atheists have staked out the claim that evolution is on such a solid foundation that it is no longer a theory, but rather a fact. They are absolutely opposed to any creation theory being taught in

public schools. On the opposite side sit the creationists who insist
adamantly that creation is a scientific theory which should be given at
least equal treatment in public schools along with evolution. Their
goal, usually unstated, is to remove evolution from the curriculum
and replace it with the young earth theory.[1] Out of fairness, it should
be pointed out that not all who would call themselves creationists
have such a radical agenda, but this opinion certainly represents the
view of many.

One example of this ongoing battle is the famous Scopes
"monkey" trial in Tennessee in 1925 which for the first time
indirectly allowed evolution to be taught in schools in that state. As
another example, the U.S. Supreme Court reached a decision in 1968
in the case Epperson v. Arkansas which struck down an Arkansas law
forbidding the teaching of "the theory or doctrine that mankind
ascended or descended from a lower order of animals." In these cases
as well as in the well known "Scopes II" trial in California,
politicians, creationists, scientists and religious leaders have fought
for control of the secondary school curriculum related to the origin
of man. Ronald Reagan, being the ever-astute politician that he was,
injected the debate between his religious right allies and the "liberal"
evolutionists in the 1980 presidential campaign with his statement
that evolution "is a theory, a scientific theory only, and it has in
recent years been challenged in the world of science and is not yet
believed in the scientific community to be as infallible as it once was
believed." It is true that evolution is just a theory, but hidden behind
his statement is the attempt of creationists to argue that the creationist
theory of origins is on an equal or more solid footing than evolution.

---

[1] For an example of this agenda being applied, a bill was passed by the
Arkansas legislature in 1981, which legislated the teaching of creation science in
public schools. Creation science was defined in this bill (Arkansas Statute 590) as:

(It) means the scientific evidence for creation and inferences from those
scientific evidences and related inferences that indicate: (1) Sudden creation of the
universe, energy and life from nothing. (2) The insufficiency of mutation and natural
selection in bringing about development of all living kinds from a single organism.
(3) Changes only within fixed limits of originally created kinds of plants and animals.
(4) Separate ancestry for man and apes. (5) Explanation of the earth's geology by
catastrophism, including the occurrence of a worldwide flood. (6) A relatively recent
inception of the earth and living kinds. This legislation was later found to be
unconstitutional. Author's note: Points one through three can be supported from
science, and perhaps point four as well, but points five and six are what makes this a
"radical agenda," at least in the opinion of the author.

In the first part of this section, the theory of evolution will be defined. Next, the evidence in support of this theory will be briefly discussed. Following that, a possible alternative view for understanding the origin of species will be presented along with a discussion of how all this relates to the contents of the Bible.

The discussion of evolution has been left to a separate and later chapter of the book for two reasons. First, although evolution and its relationship to the Bible is a very interesting subject, it seems that the debate over evolution is not central to the themes of this book—the existence of God and the inspiration of the Bible. As to the existence of God, it has already been shown beyond a reasonable doubt that both the universe and life were created. Whether God created one life form at some distant point in the past and let it "evolve" from there according to the wisdom of his natural laws, or whether God created all the life forms visible today only a few thousand years ago—either way, God created life!

The fact is that the theory of evolution explains, not how life came to be, but rather how the original form or forms of life have changed over time. The existence of life is a miracle, plain and simple. How much created life has changed through evolution is to be discovered through studying fossil and genetic evidence.

As to how evolution relates to the inspiration of the Bible, evolution is not exactly one of its major themes. Outside of the first chapter in Genesis the origin of species is not discussed. The relationship between Genesis one and evolution will be dealt with presently, but in view of the overwhelming evidence in support of the inspiration of the Bible, some of it presented in this book, it seems unwise to base our belief or lack of belief in the Bible solely on a debatable interpretation of one passage.

Second, although I am a trained scientist, my personal expertise is in physics and chemistry, not biology (as mentioned before, my Ph.D. is in chemical physics). The origin of the universe is a question of physics primarily, while the origin of life is a question of chemistry primarily. Evolution is a question primarily of biology. Having never taken a course in genetics or evolutionary biology, I would be considered a layperson in these areas. Although I have studied the question of evolution carefully, the fact that I am not an expert should be considered when reading the following.

Life was created by God. As stated above, the theory of evolution provides one model to explain how the original life form or forms have changed since their creation to produce the myriad of life forms that exist on the earth today. In the words of Charles Darwin:

> It is mere rubbish thinking at present of the origin of life. One might as well think of the origin of matter.

The origin of the first life-forms, whether they be one-celled or very advanced—whether there were many original forms or one, the evolutionist will have a difficult time ultimately deciding, because evolution is not a theory of origins. Rather, evolution is a theory of changes. Apparently at one point in his career, Darwin, the originator of the theory of evolution seemed to be unsure himself about how the original species came to be.

The theory of evolution, with all the implications required for the atheist to be able to accept it might be simply stated as follows:

> The original one-celled life form, through mutation and subsequent genetic variation, under the influence of natural selection has produced all the life forms which now exist or have ever existed on the earth.

This claim is either true or it is not. It will either hold up to scientific criticism and the evidence or it will not. The claim will be investigated, along with its relationship to the Bible.

EVIDENCE FOR EVOLUTION

First consider the evidence in support of the evolutionary theory. There are two principal bodies of evidence which can be used in support of the theory of evolution. They are:

1. Genetics

2. The fossil record

This is an oversimplification, but sufficient for a starting point. Contrary to popular belief, genetics supply the strongest evidence in support of evolution. Those who would seek to "disprove" evolution typically attack the evidence from the fossil record rather than that from genetics. The goal here is not to attack or even to disprove evolution. However, any attempt to do either should discuss the genetic evidence in support of evolution.

The basic idea of genetics is that each generation of a species inherits its traits from its parent or parents through the DNA molecules contained in its chromosomes. When biologists analyze the DNA in mammals, for example, they find that all mammals have similar DNA, providing strong support for the idea that the different species of mammals are all genetically related, and therefore perhaps all evolved from some original "mammal."

The logical implication of evolution is that species which are closely related by descent should have similar DNA. This law, although perhaps not perfectly adhered to, generally proves true. For example, The DNA in chimpanzees has about a 99% similarity to that of humans. Logically (at least according to the logic of evolution), crocodiles should have DNA less similar to that of humans than chimpanzees to humans. On the other hand, ostriches should have more similarity in their DNA to hummingbirds than to lobsters. When the DNA evidence is examined, although there might be some interesting surprises, the general implications of evolution for genetics prove true.

To those who are emotionally tied in to the idea that Adam and Eve were created (the author would count himself among them) this sort of information may incite a reaction. Facts are facts however, and the fact is that studies of the DNA in plants and animals, at least on the surface, is consistent with the theory of organic evolution.

The second chief type of evidence called upon to support the evolutionary theory is from the fossil record. It is interesting that although the science of genetics was developed by Gregor Mendel in 1865, at about the same date as the original edition of Darwin's Origin of Species, his theory of genetics was not generally given serious consideration until the early twentieth century. Therefore, Darwin did not use the evidence from genetics to support his theory at all. He primarily referred to the evidence from the fossil record as well as the apparent adaptation of living species to their environment. To quote Darwin:

> The great principle of evolution stands up clear and firm, when these groups of facts are considered in connection with others, such as the mutual affinities of the members of the same group, their geographical distribution in past and present times, and their *geological succession*. It is

incredible that all these facts should speak falsely. He who
is not content to look, like a savage, at the phenomena of
nature as disconnected, cannot any longer believe that man
is the work of a separate act of creation.[2] (emphasis added)

By "geological succession," Darwin means from fossil evidence.
Darwin is claiming here, and evolutionists have followed his lead,
that when one looks at the fossil evidence, one will find a gradual
change from more ancient species to more modern ones. This is
illustrated by the familiar evolutionary family tree which will show
for example, mammals and birds evolving from reptiles, which in
turn evolved from amphibians, which evolved from fish and so forth
back to the most ancient single-cell ancestors.

Creationists have certainly cried foul at this point: but not just
creationists. Legitimate science has often and consistently called into
question this claim, asking for evidence of missing links and certain
hard-to-imagine in-between evolutionary forms. A statement of the
famous orator William Jennings Bryan given at the Scopes trial,
although perhaps a bit overstated, would represent this view:

> Today there is not a scientist in all the world who can
> trace one single species to any other, and yet they call us
> ignoramuses and bigots because we do not throw away our
> Bible and accept it is proved that out of two or three million
> species not a one is traceable to another. And they say that
> evolution is a fact when they cannot prove that one species
> came from another, and if there is such a thing, all species
> must have come, commencing as they say, commencing in
> that one lonely cell down there in the bottom of the ocean
> that just evolved and evolved until it got to be a man. And
> they cannot find a single species that came from another,
> and yet they demand that we allow them to teach this stuff
> to our children, that they may come home with their
> imaginary family tree and scoff at their mother's and
> father's Bible.

The question of succession of species and the related question of
missing links is a difficult one, but the evolutionist would defend
their position as follows. Yes, it is true that the succession of separate

---

[2] Charles Darwin, *The Descent of Man*, 1871.

species cannot be demonstrated in the laboratory, and yes it is true that significant "gaps" in the fossil record exist. Nevertheless, with the passage of time and as the body of evidence increases, new data consistently tends to fill in the gaps and to support the general claims of evolution. If the theory of evolution were without any validity, then one might assume that as evidence is collected it would tend to make the theory less and less believable. The converse is true. With increasing data, the theory of evolution has in general become more plausible, not less.

To conclude this brief exposition on the data in support of evolution (remember that there are significant questions to be asked of the evolutionary theory as well, some of which will be presented presently), the fact is that the chief predictions of the evolutionary theory are more or less consistent with known fact. As data continues to come in, rather than providing more reason to doubt evolution, it tends to support it. Notice the word *tends* is used here, because it will be shown that there is a significant body of evidence which calls into question many of the assumptions of the evolutionary theory.

ANOTHER MODEL

Having given evolutionary theory a fair hearing, it would be appropriate to consider another viewpoint. The theory of evolution has itself evolved to deal with some difficult questions. The first of these is the question of the mode of evolution. How do new species come about? How does a species with 46 chromosomes evolve from a different species with 34 chromosomes? The concept of natural selection assumes genetic variety in a population and "natural selection" of the traits most suited to the specific environment. The question is where does this variety come from?

Geneticists would mention genetic mutations as the source of variations in the gene pool. Mutations do indeed occur, but the vast majority of them are not at all beneficial. The probability of a single mutation being beneficial has been estimated as low as one in a million. Since mutations are virtually always harmful, the skeptic would claim that they cannot possibly help species to "evolve" to higher species. This is a good point. It is relatively easy to imagine the world population of mosquitoes, presumably in the trillions, having enough numbers to evolve through mutation around a particular environmental difficulty. It is more difficult to imagine a particular species of whales, numbering in only the thousands using mutation to survive an environmental change.

Evolutionists, of course, have come up with attempts to explain how this process occurs. The fact is, however, that the means by which genetic diversity occurs and its relationship to natural selection is still very much in doubt. Evolutionary theory has proven to be very flexible. Historically it has been adapted in response to whatever criticisms have been raised. Nevertheless, a convincing model to explain the origin of genetic diversity is still lacking.

This brings out one significant point about the theory of evolution. It is by its very nature impossible to prove or to disprove evolution. The theory uses data from the distant past to explain events of the distant past. Despite the confident claims of evolutionists that evolution is "proved," in the end it can never be proven. For example, it is simply impossible to "prove" that birds evolved from dinosaurs, as has been claimed more and more strongly lately. (By the way, most ornithologists hotly contest the claim that birds evolved from dinosaurs, despite what was shown in the movie *Jurassic Park*). The process, if it occurred, certainly cannot be repeated in the laboratory, so the normal method scientists use to verify a scientific theory is not available.

On the other hand, evolution can never be disproved scientifically either. Because it is a theory primarily about the past, the proponents of evolution theory need only adapt the theory to fit as well as possible the available data from the past. It is worth remembering that a great number of evolutionists are committed to the theory at least in part because they have assumed, before even beginning the investigation, that every phenomenon in the natural world has a natural, rather than a supernatural explanation. Despite the confident claims of creationists and others that evolution has been disproved, this goal will probably prove elusive.

To summarize again the case for evolution, there exists data from genetics, from the fossil record, from embryology, from population distributions and so forth, all of which seem to support, at least in its broad outline the evolution model. The question is whether there is any other model consistent with the scientific evidence.

Before moving on to other models for the origin of species, consider the question referred to above which evolutionists have struggled to answer. This question arises when one looks at the fossil record. Evolutionary theory would predict a slow and gradual change of species over many millions of years. That certainly is what Darwin had in mind. Evolutionists have been unable to predict the rate of change from their models. Instead, they seek to create a model consistent with the data. This is the reverse of the normal process of science.

When one looks at the actual fossil record, one finds information *dramatically* in contradiction to what would seem to be the logical implications of the evolutionary theory of a slow and fairly gradual change of species. In fact, the fossil record shows evidence of *extremely* rapid change on a geological time scale. When the fossil record is examined, species seem to make great leaps of change or even to appear seemingly out of nowhere in virtually zero time geologically, followed by long periods with very little change.

Upon a careful examination, the fossil record does show some long periods of relatively small and gradual change, consistent with the broad idea of the evolutionary theory. However, at certain times in the past, events have occurred after which as much as ninety percent of all species have disappeared, followed by dramatically new species seeming to appear almost as if out of nowhere.

The most famous of these dramatic die-offs and new species creations is called the Cambrian catastrophe or the Cambrian explosion, depending on whether one wants to refer to the species die-off or the new species creation. To quote from an article entitled The Big Bang of Animal Evolution:[3]

> Nevertheless, compared with the context of the 3.5 billion years of all biological history and the roughly 570 million years since the start of the Cambrian, the phyla do seem to have appeared *suddenly* and *simultaneously*. For that reason, some paleontologists refer to the Cambrian "explosion"...This evidence seems to confirm that there was a spectacular evolutionary radiation in the early Cambrian....Cambrian explosion was characterized by the *sudden* and roughly *simultaneous* appearance of many diverse animal forms almost 600 million years ago (emphasis added).

There it is. Although slow and gradual change does seem to occur when the fossil record is viewed (for example, the famous

---

[3] Jeffery S. Levinton, *Scientific American*, November 1992, p. 84.

series of horse fossils appears to illustrate this), the evidence shows that the most significant "changes" in life forms on the earth have occurred in a series of sudden and simultaneous events. As noted in the article quoted above, all the animal phyla with hard parts arose during this Cambrian explosion. In the subsequent 570 million years, no new hard body part patterns have appeared. This Cambrian event is not unique, although it is the most striking example. Another die-off and subsequent dramatic and sudden species appearance occurred in the Permian period, 230 million years ago. In this event, as much as 96 percent of all species disappeared and many new species suddenly appeared. It should be noted that this is not an idea from paleontologists on the fringe of the field. This is a thoroughly documented finding of which all evolutionists are well aware.

Of course, evolutionists attempt to explain the data. To quote the above-mentioned article:[4]

> Evolutionary biologists are still trying to determine why no new body plans have appeared during the past half a billion years....One idea worth entertaining is that evolution occurs more slowly today than it did when the earth was young....I have argued that at least part of the answer may depend on the evolution of commitment to a developmental program....In response to natural selection pressures, developmental programs may evolve to restrict the degree of change in successful body plans. We can only speculate about what genetic mechanisms might permanently set development...

This is an article by a main-line evolutionist. The proposal is astounding! The rate of evolution is said to be variable. Evolution may have a "commitment to a developmental program." The author should be given leeway in using familiar terminology to describe an unfamiliar occurrence, but this is surprising language for an evolutionist to use to say the least. If there is a development plan, it would certainly seem reasonable to assume that there is a planner at the head of development! That planner, of course, is God.

It can be predicted that evolutionists will devise a model, however speculative, to explain the facts. The question is, does the atheistic model of the origin of the species serve as the best model to

---

[4] ibid., pp. 87,90.

explain the data? In the final analysis it does not.

Life was created. As stated before, the only question is whether God created one original life form or many. The evidence above speaks strongly for the idea that God has created many different life forms at different times. The evidence points to various divergent species appearing "suddenly and simultaneously" at different points in the past. Here the hand of God can be seen. The picture created by scientific evidence is consistent with the creation of different species at different times, followed by a slow and gradual evolution of these species from that point.

Although this model is consistent with the fossil evidence, it could be predicted that it will not find its way into biology textbooks any time soon. This is partly because of the atheistic/naturalistic bias of the textbook writers. The non-believer assumes that a miraculous event cannot happen, therefore they will not give serious attention to this model, no matter how compellingly the evidence supports it. To tell the truth, even a scientist who is open to this idea might struggle to put it into their science text because a creation event is something science does not know how to deal with. Even a scientist who believes in multiple strands of creation followed by evolution might mention it in class, but not include it in their textbooks, as that idea would not strictly be "science."

The evidence from the fossil record pointing to simultaneous massive destructions and creations of species is not the only area that has caused even many committed evolutionists to take a good hard look at their models.

For example, the theory of evolution requires very gradual changes of species over time. This is true because the only known natural means of creating genetic diversity is through mutation. As mentioned before, it has been estimated that somewhere around a million mutations are required before even one would occur which might prove eventually beneficial. However, in order for one species to "evolve" into another, many thousands of such beneficial mutations would have to occur. It was stated above that apes are approximately 99% similar in genetic material to humans. What was not mentioned is that there are about one billion pieces of genetic information contained in that material. Using that number, even a change of one percent in genetic information would require ten million beneficial or at least non-harmful mutations. How long would this take to happen? How many generations would be required, and how many simultaneous changes can happen at once? For the atheistic theory of evolution to be supported, these questions must be answered.

As another example, consider the eye of the trilobite, a very primitive and relatively simple species (by comparison to humans) which appeared right at the Cambrian explosion. Some trilobites were blind, but some had an incredible eye. Unlike the flexible lenses in the eyes of mammals the eye of the trilobite was formed in its upper half of a very hard crystal of the mineral calcite. In this part of the eye, a large number of separate mini-crystals were stacked together in such a way that they produced a perfect focus at the back of the eye, where apparently there were nerve receptors to receive the image. To make this even more amazing, the lower part of the lens was composed of the hard organic material called chitin, which also had a shape that could focus light at the same point as the upper part. This amazing double lens had the property of eliminating what physicists call spherical aberration. Spherical aberration is a problem which spherical lenses have in producing a focused image. Even the human eye has this problem, but not the wonderfully designed eye of the trilobite. Its double lens eliminates this problem.

The question to be asked is how many beneficial mutations had to occur for this eye to form where there was no eye before? Surely it would involve thousands of mutations. Remember, the genetic code had to be created which could produce the calcite crystals in just the precisely correct shape, along with separate genetic information which could make the chitin part of the lens. Not only that, but unless the beneficial genetic mutations (hundreds or thousands of them) which could produce the nerve cells to detect the light happened simultaneously, what good would all these supposedly beneficial mutations be?

Remember that the trilobite appeared in the fossil record in virtually no time on a geological scale with no obvious predecessor. It did not just have a new eye, it had a very large number of other new features. Let the evolutionist be completely honest with this question. How did this happen? Perhaps it is unfair to ask for a complete explanation, but the idea of many thousands of coordinated beneficial mutations (which would not even be beneficial unless they occurred in parallel) begs an explanation of some sort. Again, according to the fossil record, such changes must happen very rapidly. A noted evolutionist Gordan Rattray Taylor said concerning this example:[5]

> By what conceivable chance could the trilobite have
> accumulated the one material in the universe—namely
> calcite—which had the required optical properties, and then
> imposed on it the one type of curved surface which would
> achieve the required result?...We are still reeling at the
> improbability of this.

Taylor was at one time the chief science adviser for the BBC. He
was not a believer in special creation at all, but rather an evolutionist.
However, his studies led him to believe that the Darwinian model
simply cannot explain the evidence. For the interested reader, Taylor
lists many similar examples in his book.

It is interesting to note that Charles Darwin himself, in *Origin of
Species* said concerning the origin of the human eye:

> To suppose that the origin of the eye, with all its
> inimitable contrivances for adjusting the focus to different
> distances could have been formed by natural selection,
> seems, I freely confess, absurd in the highest possible
> degree.

He was quoted later in life as saying "The eye gives me a cold
shudder." There are an innumerable number of examples along these
lines which can be mentioned.[6] In fact, the lack of transitional forms
in the fossil record between species has prompted Stephen Jay Gould,
one of the most respected evolutionists of our day, to make the
following statements.[7]

> New fossils almost always appeared suddenly in the
> fossil record with no intermediate links to ancestors in the
> older rocks of the same region (p. 12).

---

[5] Gordon Rattray, *The Great Evolution Mystery* (Taylor, Secher and Warburg,
London, 1983), p. 98.

[6] A very good treatment of this subject, considerably more thorough than is
provided here, can be found in Alan Hayward, *Creation and Evolution* (Bethany
House Publishers, Minneapolis, Minnesota, 1995), pp. 13-53.

[7] Stephen Jay Gould, "Evolution's Erratic Pace," *Natural History*, Vol. 5, May,
1977.

The extreme rarity of transitional forms in the fossil record persists as the trade secret of paleontology. The evolutionary trees that adorn our textbooks have data only at the tips and nodes of their branches; the rest is inference, however reasonable, not the evidence of fossils...We fancy ourselves as the only true students of life's history, yet to preserve our favored account of evolution by natural selection we view our data as so bad that we never see the very process we profess to study" (p. 14).

Gould is definitely not a believer in creation, but he points out that the fossil evidence is in dramatic contrast to the natural predictions of the evolutionary model as it is normally used.

Another well-known scientist who has applied mathematics to study the theory of evolution is Sir Fred Hoyle, a professed agnostic. Hoyle has attempted to model the probability of beneficial mutations along with estimations of the number of simultaneous beneficial mutations required for species to evolve from one another. He concluded that:[8]

The general scientific world has been bambooozled into believing that evolution has been proved. Nothing could be farther from the truth.

In the same book, he makes the bold statement regarding his study of mutations and their relation to speciation, "These conclusions dispose of Darwinism."

Another physicist, H. S. Lipson, performed similar calculations, which were published in the *Physics Bulletin*.[9] He concluded that:

We must go further than this and admit that the only acceptable alternative is creation. I know that this is anathema to physicists, as indeed it is to me, but we must not reject a theory that we do not like if the experimental evidence supports it.

Lipson is not at all a creationist, but his willingness to make a

[8] F. Hoyle and N. C. Wickramasinghe, *Evolution from Space* (Simon and Schuster, New York, 1981).

[9] H. S. Lipson, *Physics Bulletin*, **30**, 1979, p. 140, **31**, 1980, p. 138, and **31**, 1980, p. 337.

statement like this openly is admirable. He is simply stating that the level of improbability for the evolution of species by today's models forces him to at least admit the possibility of special creation.

One could easily quote many examples of organs which exist in nature which, when examined carefully, require such a mind-boggling number of simultaneous beneficial mutations that evolutionists find themselves grasping for terms such as "positive evolutionary principle" or "evolutionary plan" to describe them.

Considering this, and considering that the fossil record in places such as the Cambrian explosion shows massive and sudden appearance of new species, seemingly out of nowhere, the open minded person is forced to consider a radically different model from the current Darwinian or neo-Darwinian evolutionary theories.

The author would conclude that the most reasonable explanation of the fossil record is that the Creator has produced a number of different species at different times in the past. After creating these species, it would appear that God has allowed them to "evolve" gradually into the forms which may be observed today. A majority of scientists will obviously resist this model because it invokes a supernatural event, but it seems to be the only model that can explain the data.

This rather bold claim brings up a question. If one accepts this model it is reasonable to ask why the Creator would spend hundreds of millions of years creating life as we now see it. Does this mean he is not really so powerful? Why did God not get the whole process of creation over within a short period of time? Is he just slow? It would seem difficult to give a conclusive answer to this question. All that can be said is that the evidence points to this explanation. The scientists quoted above stated that they could only speculate about the genetic mechanisms which might create these sudden species appearances. Similarly, one can only speculate about why God chose to create the world over such a long period of time, using a mixture of divine and natural processes.

If one allows for the intervention of God in the formation of species to explain the evidence for rapid changes and sudden appearances of species, then what about the more gradual types of evolution which are observable from the fossil record? This kind of change, sometimes called microevolution, is observable by scientists. The best-documented cases are the apparent evolution of bacteria and viruses in response to environmental stresses such as the use of antibiotics. If extremely rapid changes and sudden appearances of species (macroevolution) has a divine explanation, then it seems perfectly reasonable to conjecture that God has a hand in every step of the process of evolution. Perhaps there is some process by which the divine being influences even the most minute but favorable genetic change. Admittedly, this is speculation, but the question seems to be not so much whether or not God has intervened in the origin of species, but rather how much and how often he intercedes. What is being described here is sometimes called "theistic evolution." Does a proper reading of the Bible allow for theistic evolution? Is this the most reasonable (though admittedly by the strict definition not scientific) explanation of how species change? Let the reader decide.

Two conclusions, then, remain. First, life was created. Second, the scientific evidence points to various divergent species being created at different times. Apparently these species were created according to a "developmental program." It would appear that they were created according to a common genetic pattern as well. The building blocks of all species are essentially similar. Although different created species have different DNA molecules, they all have much in common in their genetic code because they were created according to a pattern. Two of God's creations with more in common in their outward form would seem to have more in common genetically. This is in fact what happens to be seen in the natural world.

This model is not inconsistent with the thinking of early evolutionists. Many hesitated to speculate about the origins of life. At one time Darwin considered the idea of a number of original species from which evolution occurred. An early evolutionist when considering this question said:

> If we begin, as it were, at the other end and trace things backwards from the present, instead of forwards from the remote past, it cannot be denied that Darwin's investigations have made it exceedingly probable that the vast variety of plants and animals have sprung from a much smaller number of original forms.[10]

---

[10] Frederick Temple, *The Relations Between Religion and Science*, (Macmillan and Company, London, 1884).

Here the author, an evolutionist, saw an unspecified number of original forms. It was only when later evolutionists attempted to come up with a theory which was avowedly naturalistic—one which did not necessitate invoking a divine creator—that this idea of multiple original forms came to fall out of favor. Given the most recent fossil evidence, it is time to recall the multiple original form idea to the evolution debate.

The believer who prefers to interpret the first chapter of Genesis literally would object. This person would point out that the creation account describes six days of creation, not hundreds of millions of years. A case has already been made for not necessarily interpreting Genesis chapter one in its most literal sense. However, the point is not how to interpret Genesis chapter one; the point is to ask what model is consistent with the evidence. The model described above fits that criterion. As stated before, God certainly could have created the earth with an appearance of age, and perhaps he did. If he did, science would not have much to say about it. All that has been done here is to present a model consistent with the available data.

But this brings the story back to Genesis chapter one as promised. The Genesis account of creation involves different species being created at different times ("days"). "So God created the great creatures of the sea and every living and moving thing with which the water teems, according to their kinds, and every winged bird according to its kind" (Genesis 1:21). Given the evidence already shown in this book, it is not surprising that the account in Genesis is consistent with the model proposed above, which in turn is consistent with the best scientific evidence available today.

CONCLUSION

In summary, although those committed to the creationist's line of thinking would like to create the impression that the evolutionary theory is just a paper tiger which will fall apart with the slightest scientific scrutiny, this is simply not the case. The data available from science is, on the whole, consistent with evolutionary theory. However, when one looks closely at the origin of species, and at the fossil record, one will discover that the form of evolutionary theory to which the atheist must ascribe struggles to explain genetic diversity. It also cannot easily explain the fossil record, which shows dramatic evidence of divergent species appearing suddenly. A model more consistent with the genetic diversity and the sudden appearance of dramatically divergent species is one which allows for different species being created at different times, followed by more gradual change. This model is in a sense not "scientific" in that it invokes supernatural events. However, given that it has already been shown the laws of nature imply life itself must have been created, this model becomes more believable. This model is also consistent with the outline of the creation account in the Bible.

THE ORIGIN OF MAN

The second question to be brought up in this chapter is the origin of man. How did the human race originate? This question is obviously very closely related to the question of evolution discussed above. This was the real issue behind the Scopes monkey trial. Did man evolve from apes? Or is humanity a special creation of God?

It has already been shown that life was created. It can also be seen that the fossil and genetic evidence is consistent with a model which allows for different species having been created at different times in the past. But what about man? Did man evolve from a lower form, or is he one of those created species? This is clearly a highly emotionally charged question for many people. The first question which should be asked is what does the evidence say?

Probably almost every adult American has seen by now the familiar pictures from one of the many National Geographic series on the evolution of man. They show a series of species, beginning in the fairly remote past, gradually standing more erect, gradually having a more pronounced forehead and presumably larger brain. The next-to last picture is the *Neandertal* (also known as *Neanderthal*), followed by the *Cro Magnon*, modern man. The implication is clear. A statement from the National Academy of Sciences brings out the full implications of this picture.

> Studies in evolutionary biology have led to the conclusion that mankind arose from ancestral primates. This association was hotly debated among scientists in Darwin's day, before molecular biology and the discovery of the now abundant links. Today, however, there is no significant scientific doubt about the close evolutionary relationships among all primates or between apes and

humans. The "missing links" that troubled Darwin and his followers are no longer missing. Today, not one but many such connecting links, intermediate between various branches of the primate family tree, have been found as fossils.[11]

This statement is a dramatic overstatement of the facts, but it would typify the view of many scientists, especially those who are atheists.

So what are these "links," and what do they prove? Consider an outline of the evidence as well as the conclusions of anthropologists from this evidence. In Darwin's day there was virtually no direct evidence that man evolved from apes. Presumably Darwin made the claim based on faith in his theory as well as the relatively similar anatomical form of apes and humans. Since that time, some evidence regarding proposed links between apes and humans has been discovered. These discoveries are worth listing.

One proposed link is the species known as *Australopithecus afarensis*. This species is conjectured to have lived from about four million years ago until about one million years ago. The most famous *afarensis* find is known as Lucy. This fossil find was made in 1976. However, it is missing a skull, the most important part of the skeleton for making comparisons to human features. Since the discovery of Lucy, over three hundred fossil finds have been classified as being afarensis. Most of these are fragmentary—a part of a jaw or a few teeth and the like. However, in 1992 a nearly complete skull identified as *afarensis* was discovered. Other proposed links have been discovered and identified as distinct from *Australopithecus afarensis*. These include *Homo erectus*, proposed to have lived from about one million to a few hundred thousand years ago. Conjectured to be distinct from this species is "archaic" *Homo sapiens*, proposed to have lived from a few hundred thousand years ago until about two hundred thousand years ago. The distinctions between these species are hotly debated among anthropologists, and it can be assumed that the current labels will change with time as new discoveries are made.[12]

---

[11] *Science and Creationism: A View from the National Academy of Sciences,* 1984, National Academy Press, Washington, DC.

[12] Several recent National Geographic articles present some of the evidence discussed here in a very readable form. These include articles in the September 1995,

On a more solid footing is the more recent *Neandertal*. Specimens identified as *Neandertal* have been dated from about two hundred fifty thousand years in the past to about forty thousand years ago (these numbers are vigorously debated as well). Unlike the species mentioned above, there is a wealth of evidence concerning *Neandertals*. Hundreds of skeletons have been identified. Most recent of all is the fossils known popularly as *Cro Magnon*. Most anthropologists would concur that *Cro Magnon* is modern Homo sapiens. In other words they are people.

So what about the evidence? As one looks at the skeletal remains, one sees ape, ape, ape, people, and people. The first three species named above were all clearly apes. They all had arm hand and leg features of apes. The major distinction between these apes and modern chimpanzees and gorillas is that their hip structure would imply they might have moved about mainly by walking upright. Anthropologists hotly debate even this conclusion. They all had brain sizes about one third that of modern humans, the same size, more or less, as modern apes. On the other hand, *Neandertal* had brains on average slightly larger than modern man's. They had significantly different muscle structure and facial bone structure on average, but if dressed up carefully, they could pass as modern man. They used fire, they made tools and built simple living structures.

Please bear in mind that the writer of all this is not an expert in the field. As mentioned, I am a chemist and a physicist. The interested reader should read up on this subject in order to reach his or her own conclusion. Find an anthropologist and talk to them. Be skeptical but open-minded and ask questions.

It is time to relate the evidence to what is found in the Bible. Biologists would claim that man appeared gradually by evolution from a half-ape/half-human ancestor. What does the Bible have to say about this? To answer the question, one must return to the book of Genesis. The creation of Adam and Eve is recorded in Genesis chapters one and two. "So God created man in his own image, in the image of God he created him." (Genesis 1:27) "And the Lord God formed man (Adam) from the dust of the ground and breathed into his nostrils the breath of life, and man became a living being." (Genesis 2:7)

According to the Bible, man was created. He did not evolve

from apes. It is hard to imagine interpreting these scriptures any other way. Some, in an attempt to reconcile the Bible with the scientific evidence, have taken the creation of Adam and Eve to be an allegory to describe in the most general terms the creation and fall of man. Others have speculated that God took an already-evolved being and simply imbued that creature with spiritual qualities to make man in his own image. Perhaps these explanation should not be dogmatically ruled out, but it should be conceded that throughout the Bible, the story of Adam and Eve seems to be taken as fact.

So what about the evidence? It has already been shown that life was created. It has also been suggested in the previous section, using evidence from the fossil record, that God has created many different species at different times. It is not a great stretch to imagine that God could have created man.

There is a very important point to be made about this however. The bottom line is that belief in mankind as a separate supernatural creation of God is based at least partly, if not mostly, on faith. The strongest reason to believe the creation of man was by miraculous means is because the Bible says so. Remember that it is important to separate what is believed by faith from what is believed primarily because of the evidence. A conviction that the Bible is inspired by God would lead to a conviction about heaven. It would also lead to confidence that Jesus Christ will come back some day. It is also part of the reason to believe the Adam and Eve account.

It is true that the evidence from paleontology points to ape, ape, ape, man, man. It so happens that this is not in conflict with the Biblical account, claiming that man was created. However, this is not the same as being able to claim that the belief that man evolved is ridiculous. Although the ascent of man from apes is far from proven, it is not an outrageous leap from the evidence either. In fact I would be so bold as to admit that if it were not for what is recorded in the Bible, I would probably have accepted the evolutionist's conclusion about the origins of man. The theory of the evolution of man from apes is a virtual religion to many such as the Leakys. Their zeal may cause them to be overconfident in their claims.

One could justify calling into question the accuracy of the dating of *afarensis* and other fossils. Many times scientists have ended up red-faced because they were not sufficiently skeptical about unproved theories. Nevertheless, the fact is that as evidence has been accumulated, it has lent more credence, not less, to the claim of the evolutionists in this area.

In summary, one is left with an unproven theory of human origins—a theory which is unproven but which has enough supporting evidence to make it believable. One is also left with a Biblical claim that man was created—a claim which does not conflict with the scientific evidence. Acceptance of the Biblical claim that man was a special creation amounts to a belief in the supernatural—a belief that science cannot explain every event that has ever occurred. For reasons too numerous to list, I believe the Bible is inspired by God. I believe in the Biblical account of creation.

For Today

1. What ideas about evolution and the origin of man did you bring in to reading this book?

2. Have any of your beliefs been changed or at least challenged by what you have read?

3. Do you believe the creationist's theories about the origin of species and of man should be taught in science classes on an equal footing with evolution? Why or why not?

4. Whether you believe in it or not, can you summarize the evidence which supports the theory of evolution in a few sentences?

5. How does evidence from the fossil record, such as that of the pre-Cambrian explosion relate to the question of the origin of species?

6. Assuming that you believe the account of Adam and Eve (presumably a big assumption for some of the readers), do you believe the account because of evidence to support it, or because it is recorded in the Bible and you just happen to have faith in the accuracy of the Bible?

*The first to present his case seems
right, till another comes forward and
questions him.*

Proverbs 18:17

9

WILL IT BE FIRE NEXT TIME?

The last question which will be considered is the flood. The Bible in Genesis chapters six through eight describes a great flood of apparently worldwide scope. Did this flood actually happen? Is the story just a myth, or perhaps less argumentatively, is it just a parable about the nature of man? These questions will be considered in this chapter. It might be a good idea to read the account in Genesis before continuing this chapter. To sum it up, a few quotes from Genesis 7:7-23 are provided which will make the point about the nature of this flood as described in the Bible.

> For forty days the flood kept coming on the earth....The waters rose and covered the mountains to a depth of more than fifteen cubits*... Everything on dry land that had the breath of life in its nostrils died...Only Noah was left, and those with him on the ark.

*A cubit is about eighteen inches.

A few questions present themselves immediately. When did this flood happen (if it happened)? What does the mountains being covered by twenty feet of water mean? Does it mean a total depth of twenty feet of rain or literally the highest mountaintop was twenty feet under? What about "Everything on dry land" dying? Does that mean all species had at least some members perish in this flood, or does it mean every member of every species (except those in the ark) was killed? Is there any evidence this flood actually happened?

A number of explanations of the Biblical account have been offered. The skeptic would argue that this is just another of the myths in the Bible—further proof that the Bible was written by a scientifically ignorant people. They would scoff at the idea of God speaking to Noah, and laugh at the idea of him building such a huge boat and just waiting there for all these animals to show up at his door. If it were not for the overwhelming evidence for the inspiration of the Bible, some already presented here, the skeptic would have a very good point to make. This is clearly something that does not happen every day. Animals suddenly traveling great distances and voluntarily entering a boat would be uncharacteristic to say the least. In fact it would be downright miraculous. Surely, however, the evidence of the divine origin of the Bible is sufficient to encourage one to look more closely.

At the other extreme, some in the creationist's camp would claim not only that the flood described in Genesis happened: they would claim that this flood would explain all the sedimentary deposits on the earth. In other words, creationists would use the flood to explain the worldwide sedimentary rock layers; on average thousands of feet deep. This claim has been mentioned previously. The creationists would have us believe that in this one huge, world-wide turbulent flood, the trilobites by some luck always settled out below the amphibians, which somehow managed to consistently settle below the dinosaurs, and the dinosaurs below the great mammals, all in one great cataclysmic event, producing sedimentary deposits as much as 80,000 feet deep. No more need be said about this.

Others have proposed naturalistic but pseudo-scientific explanations of the flood. One such attempt is called the "canopy" theory. This theory involves the claim that the water which fell to the earth in the flood was held in the atmosphere of the earth prior to the deluge. According to this theory, once Noah and his family entered the ark, the entire water canopy fell to earth over a forty-day period, causing the flood. There is no natural explanation for how all this water could be held up in the atmosphere. It also does not explain where the water went afterward. Did it evaporate back into the canopy? If so, why is it no longer in the sky? The theory makes no logical sense at all as a "natural" explanation.

Still others, seeking a quasi-natural explanation of the flood have proposed the "local flood" theory. They claim that somehow the flood affected only the immediate area of Mesopotamia. According to this model, all life in Mesopotamia was wiped out, but the rest of the earth was relatively unaffected. Somehow the water piled up over this one region without spilling over to neighboring regions. There is precedent for the New Testament writers using the phrase "all over the world" to refer to events which even the speaker knew did not literally affect the whole world. For example, this phrase is used in Acts 24:5 and other places. Obviously the description in Acts does not cover people in North or South America. Even as the apostle Paul spoke in Acts 24, he must have been aware that the gospel had not yet reached such little known and distant places as India and beyond. Apparently the phrase "the whole world" could be used idiomatically in the Bible. Therefore the local flood theory is not totally beyond being considered.

However, if one looks at what is described in Genesis chapters six and seven, they find a flood described which is not only world-wide, but one which lasts for hundreds of days. There could be no scientific explanation for water piling up presumably hundreds of feet for months on end in Mesopotamia without gravity causing the water to subside, unless of course the water covered the globe. The local flood would be just as miraculous as a worldwide flood, and there is no evidence for it, so why take the idea seriously?

These explanations are weak attempts to make the flood "scientific".[1] Let it be put simply: if the flood described in Genesis occurred, it was nothing short of a miracle. The flood cannot be explained by science any more than the resurrection of Jesus from the dead or his predicted return to judge the earth by fire. As is written in the New Testament (2 Peter 3:6-7),

> By water also the world of that time was deluged and destroyed. By the same word the present heavens and earth

---

[1] A more recent theory along these general lines is the "Hydroplate Theory." This is an interesting theory, which involves the floodwaters being stored in giant underground reservoirs, which are suddenly released in a cataclysmic event, which brought on the flood. However, in the opinion of the author, it falls in the same category as the others. A well-written description of this theory can be found in Walt Brown, *In the Beginning* (Center for Scientific Creation, Phoenix, 1995, www.creationscience.com).

are reserved for fire, being kept for the day of judgment and destruction of ungodly men.

There is no conceivable *scientific* explanation for the flood, any more than there will be for the earth's destruction by fire. These are acts of an omnipotent God in response to the condition of men.

According to the Bible, the flood occurred, not because of some natural law, but because of man's sin. It is stated in Genesis 6:6-8 that "The Lord was grieved that he had made man on the earth, and his heart was filled with pain." There is some evidence for the flood having occurred, as will be shown. In fact, if the flood occurred, it seems reasonable to expect that some remnant sign would remain. These signs will be described, but let it be remembered that although there is some tantalizing evidence to support the idea that a world-wide flood did indeed occur in the distant past, ultimately belief in the Genesis account of that flood is based on faith in the Bible. Many people are convinced that there is a day of judgement in store for all, as described in the Bible. One of the reasons to believe in a future day of judgement is that God has already judged the earth by water.

Belief in the flood, then, is ultimately based on faith, not on science. Nevertheless, it might be worthwhile considering the evidence for this worldwide flood.

First, consider what physical signs would be left behind if the flood did indeed occur. If the Genesis flood occurred, then one can assume that the water rose to great levels over the course of forty days. Think carefully what the physical evidence would be. Presumably there would have been considerable erosion. On the other hand, once the water covered a particular area, the erosion would stop, as water would no longer be flowing downhill. Also, there would be a significant amount of mud left behind, especially in lower-lying areas.

The question is whether this flood would leave unmistakable signs thousands of years later. The flood described in Genesis would cause erosion, but in most cases, no more erosion than might normally have occurred in a few years or at most a few hundred years in any one place. Mud layers would be left behind, but no more than a few feet or at most a few tens of feet. After all, the material loosened by a flood—even a massive one—would be much of the topsoil of the earth as well as some larger loose material which could be redistributed. There is not enough topsoil available to leave hundreds of feet anywhere. So much for the creationist claim that the thousands of feet of sedimentary layers are due to the flood.

In point of fact, if one looked for signs of a world-wide flood which presumably occurred thousands of years ago it is not clear that any sign would be left behind about which one could say: "Aha! There is solid proof that the flood described in Genesis occurred."

Thinking carefully about the nature of the flood described in the Bible leads one to conclude that there would be no clear-cut physical evidence that the flood occurred, assuming that God both miraculously produced and later miraculously cleared away the water. So what evidence is there that this flood actually occurred?

One evidence for a worldwide flood is in the records of cultures across the globe. Practically every ancient culture has a record of a great flood. Cultures with a flood story include the Hindus, the native cultures of Burma and of New Guinea, the aborigines of Australia, as well as the inhabitants of New Zealand. Also, there are records or stories of a great flood among the Incas and the Aztecs as well as a large number of tribes in North America. There are also flood accounts from Greece, from the Babylonians, the Japanese and the Sumerians. The Sumerians, one of the most ancient of all cultures, dated their dynasties from before "the flood" and after "the flood." In fact, when Sir Leonard Wooley excavated the ancient Sumerian city of Ur, he found an eight foot thick layer of mud and debris at the bottom of the city, below which flints and other relics of the stone-age were found.

The list could continue. In the majority of ancient cultures, on every inhabited continent, this story can be found. Interestingly, the stories are almost universally of a world-wide flood, most recording a single person or family surviving by either building a boat or going to the highest mountain peak. Theologians have claimed that the Genesis account has been borrowed from the Babylonian or Sumerian flood story. Would they claim that the Aztecs and the aborigines in Australia borrowed their stories as well?

What is the source of all these stories? They seem to have so much in common, yet many of them originated in divergent cultures in parts of the world with no known contact It is not unreasonable to assume that they are a record of an actual event in the remote past. Not unreasonable, that is, if one is willing to accept that a miraculous event, one which violates the laws of nature, can occur. No other great planet-wide event of the past left such an indelible mark as to be recorded in cultural histories across the world.

There is another piece of evidence worth mentioning. Although the flood may not have left an unambiguous sign on dry land, there is evidence of a dramatic drop in salinity in the ocean in the not-too-distant past. Geologists drilling core samples on the continental shelf of the Gulf of Mexico in the late sixties and early seventies made a surprising discovery. When analyzing the oxygen isotope ratios in the discarded shells of planktonic foraminifera in these cores, they found that there was a sudden and dramatic lowering in the salinity of the Gulf of Mexico about 11,600 years ago, followed by a gradual increase in salinity to more normal levels. In the words of Cesare Emiliani, one of the geologists who studied the samples:

> We know this, because the oxygen isotope ratios of the foraminifera shells show a marked, temporary decrease in the salinity of the waters of the Gulf of Mexico, it clearly shows there was a major period of flooding from 12,000 to 10,000 years ago. There is no question that there was a flood, and there is also no question that there was a universal flood.[2]

Emiliani is one of a number of scientist who studied these samples. Among them are James Kennett of the University of Rhode Island and Nicholas Shackleton of Cambridge University. By the way, Emiliani and the others do not conclude that this flood was the flood recorded in the Bible, but their findings are very interesting.

There are a few questions the thinking skeptic will raise. It would be a good idea to anticipate those questions. The flood, according to the account in Genesis, wiped out all people except Noah and his family. How then, the skeptic might ask, did this story survive in all these ancient cultures? How did the ancient languages, cultures and even racial features in various parts of the world survive? It is really hard to answer this question because it involves speculation. Perhaps this flood affected the whole world—every nation and all species, but did not actually, literally wipe out every one in every land. Conjecture about an event in the distant past is obviously difficult.

Along these lines, the most literal reading of the Genesis account

---

[2] Cesare Emiliani of the University of Miami, quoted in Reader's Digest, September 1977, p 133.

of the flood implies that members of every one of the millions of species on the earth was on the ark. The skeptic might legitimately ask whether Noah sailed past Australia to drop off the kangaroos, koalas and duck-billed platypuses, since they clearly could not survive hopping or waddling back to Australia. Unfortunately, there is no ready and convincing answer for these questions. Certainly God could miraculously recreate these species. Again, the flood could have been universal, but not literally complete in wiping out every single member of every species. It is simply impossible to be sure about these things. The wise person would probably keep an open mind and avoid being dogmatic concerning questions left open in the Bible.

It is worth pointing out that there have been numerous reports of expeditions to the area around Mount Ararat finding remnants of the ark. Until conclusive evidence is brought back that this discovery is genuine, it would be a good idea to be skeptical about these reports. Although the idea of finding direct archaeological evidence of Noah's ark is very tantalizing, history would tell us that it is best to withhold judgement for now. For a summary of the evidence supporting this discovery, see the book by Brown mentioned previously.

In conclusion, some things about the flood are clear and some are not. First, the Bible, with all its marks of inspiration, records a universal flood. The inspired writers of the New Testament mention the flood as a matter of historical fact. Second, there is a nearly universal record across the world of a great flood, with features remarkably similar to those described in the Bible. Third, there is also some evidence from geology that a worldwide flood did indeed happen. It will never be possible to clear up every question which might be asked about this flood, because it happened in the distant past, but the Bible believer can be confident that the flood happened. This flood serves as God's advance notice that he will return to judge the world.

By water also the world of that time was deluged and destroyed. By the same word the present heavens and earth are reserved for fire, being kept for the day of judgement and destruction of ungodly men. (2 Peter 3:6,7)

FOR TODAY

1. Do you believe the flood recorded in Genesis actually happened? Why or why not?

2. In this chapter it is claimed that a worldwide flood would not leave behind a "smoking gun." In other words, it is not clear that a great ancient flood would leave behind unambiguous physical evidence. Does this sound like a reasonable claim to you?

*For since the creation of the world
God's invisible qualities—his eternal
power and divine nature—have been
clearly seen being understand from
what has been made...*

Romans 1:20

10

COULD THIS ALL BE JUST A COINCIDENCE?

To those willing to see it that way, the physical universe and the wonders of life surely cry out that there is a creator. Truly, the words of Romans 1:20 are confirmed by virtually every aspect of the physical world. "For since the creation of the world God's invisible qualities—his eternal power and divine nature—have been clearly seen, being understood from what has been made, so that men are without excuse." Without excuse, that is, for not believing in the God who created all these things. On every level—from the submicroscopic particles of physics, to the wonders of the visible natural world, to the mind-numbing expanse of the cosmos—one can see the hand of a careful designer. The Designer created a world both practical and beautiful. Full of wonders to behold, designed to support very complicated forms of life, one can see the Creator in every aspect of the world around us. Some clear aspects of design have already been discussed, especially in the chapter on the creation of life. This chapter will describe a number of other examples in nature which point to the God who designed all these things.

One would think that if the atheistic assumption were true, then with the passage of time, and with the accumulation of scientific knowledge, it would appear more and more reasonable to assume, given what we know from science, that there is a naturalistic, rather than a divine answer for why things are the way they are. In fact, the exact opposite is the case. As physicists look at some of the facts to be described in this section, many have felt the need to propose what is now known as the *anthropic principle*. Those scientists who describe the anthropic principle have come to the conclusion that the evidence for design is so strong, that it is helpful to view the laws of nature as being designed with the specific intent of creating a universe which can support advanced forms of life. In other words, many scientists find the universe to be so finely tuned to support life that it is easier to understand and predict the laws which govern nature by simply assuming the reason the gravity force is as strong as it is, or that the electronic force is as it is, or the forces which hold nuclei together are what they are because that is what they needed to be in order to make life possible.

Atheists would scoff at the anthropic principle, of course, but the fact is that many who hold to the anthropic principle do so only quite reluctantly. Even those who do not agree that the universe was designed in order to support life often make statements which appear diametrically opposed to the atheistic assumption.

On a personal note, I was initially quite reluctant to write this chapter. Arguments from design can at times appear to use circular reasoning. Having read a number of writers on the subject, I have occasionally found myself taking the devil's advocate position when hearing arguments for creation based on evidence of design. One person's argument for design is another person's argument for a natural process.

A few years ago, I was listening to a speaker on the subject whose opinion I very much respect. In this presentation, the speaker used the arctic tern as an argument for design. At the first hearing, this argument sounds quite convincing. The arctic tern flies in an annual migration from the Arctic to the Antarctic regions and back again. This migration of the arctic tern of about 18,000 miles annually is truly amazing. The bird flies from the fringes of the Antarctic to the northernmost areas of North America in a single flight which spans about nine thousand miles. For the entire journey, the tern passes over an environment which contains nothing it is willing to eat. How, the speaker asked, did the tern learn to fly over these many thousands of miles? Why would a bird migrate thousands of miles away from any source of food? How could it by accident just happen to discover an alternative source of food so far away? The point of the speaker was that God created the arctic tern with both the ability and the knowledge required to make this amazing journey.

Probably the audience was quite convinced by this argument, and it may very well be true that in some subtle way, undetectable to science, God did indeed program the arctic tern to know how to undergo this amazing migration. To he honest, however, I find this argument unconvincing. To an evolutionary biologist, it is not difficult at all to imagine a bird which at one time migrated a relatively shorter distance; say from the central part of North America to the northern fringes of South America. This biologist might imagine the bird, for some reason having to do with ecological factors, gradually being adapted to eating types of food available in a colder environment over a number of generations. One could imagine this bird species finding it easier to obtain the type of food it wants with less competition by flying on an ever-increasing migratory route. Gradually, the bird might find itself only able to eat foods available in areas separated by a vast distance, but only available in the summer months in both the southern and northern hemispheres.

So perhaps God created the arctic tern from scratch with its amazing ability, or perhaps God took an already existing bird and programmed it to be able to make the vast migration. On the other hand, perhaps God allowed natural forces to take their course, so that the arctic tern "evolved" into what it is today. As mentioned, one person's argument for design, is another person's argument for the wonders of the working of natural systems. It seems, therefore, advisable to be skeptical of arguments for design. Great effort has been made in this book to only present arguments which will hold up to a reasonable level of skepticism. All life, including the arctic tern, reflects design, but using the great migration of the arctic tern as proof of design is not a strong argument.

A good number of the examples commonly used to prove design fall into this category. They seem good at first, but they do not hold up to careful scrutiny by people who are not inclined to believe in a supernatural designer. This fact is why I was hesitant to write a chapter specifically on design. However, upon much careful reflection on the topic, a number of arguments for design based on scientific knowledge still emerge as convincing evidence that the universe was designed to support life. As science has evolved, the growing number of examples of phenomena which seem to imply the universe was designed has spawned the ranks of scientists who hold to the anthropic principle. Some of these are discussed below.

CARBON, THE MIRACLE ELEMENT

An example of apparent design is found in the element carbon. Talk about designer jeans, carbon is a designer element! Simply stated; if carbon did not have the properties it has, there would be no life. The properties of carbon show clear evidence of design, and therefore of a creator. Why is that? To evaluate this claim, one must consider the unique properties of carbon, and why it is the only element available which can support the existence of life.

Living things are made up out of molecules. As has already been described, the molecules out of which living things are made are large and complex. For example, proteins, the molecules which control everything which occurs in cells, are made up of tens of thousands of atoms all joined together to form a complex, three-dimensional shape. The backbone of all these molecules is composed of carbon atoms. Why carbon? Of the ninety or so naturally occurring elements, carbon is the only one that has the properties which allow large, complex, three-dimensional molecules to be synthesized. The properties of carbon allow for strings of dozens and even hundreds of atoms to form. No other element has the property that long strings of the atoms of that element can form into stable molecules. Carbon can form ringed structures. It can form three-dimensional structures as well. Carbon can form single and double and triple bonds with itself and with a number of other atoms. All of these properties are unique to carbon, and all these properties are absolutely necessary for life to exist. In the words of Spock, we truly are "carbon based units."

Speaking of Star Trek, one of the original episodes of that series had Kirk and the gang coming upon a monster whose molecular structure was based on silicon. Spock said that this was very logical. The reason silicon is a "logical" alternative to carbon is that it is the only element, other than carbon, which can form a total of four bonds, and which can therefore, in principle, be used to build three-dimensional structures. Nevertheless, Spock's claim that a silicon monster is logical does not work. Silicon-silicon chemical bonds are very weak. It is impossible to build a large molecule joined together by silicon atoms. The author is sorry if the reader's faith in Star Trek is diminished, but there never has been, nor will there ever be a silicon-based life form.

Returning to the subject, if carbon did not have the properties it has, there would be no life. If you do not believe this point, please find you nearest biochemist, biologist or chemist and ask them if this claim is true. It is indisputable. There is exactly one element with the properties that allow for life to exist. Not two, one! Not zero, luckily for us. But is it luck? If some intelligent being were designing the properties of electrons, protons and neutrons, and therefore the properties of the atoms to allow for there to be living things, this being would have to create at least one element capable to making large, complex, flexible molecules. Recognizing the problem, God created carbon. Good going, God!

WATER. THE MIRACLE SOLVENT

Life requires a solvent. It requires a solvent with just exactly the properties that water happens to have. In fact, if it were not for the existence of water and its unique properties, there would be no life anywhere in the universe. This is a strong statement, but it will hold up to the strictest scrutiny. The existence of water is further evidence that there is an intelligent creator behind the scenes intent on creating life.

So, what is so special about water? I am trained as a chemist. When I teach introductory chemistry, I spend a great deal of time listing and describing all the ways in which water is a unique substance. There are so many things which are unique about water, the thought almost inevitably emerges that this really neat molecule must have been specifically designed in order to support life.

One of the special properties of water is that for a molecular substance, it is very sticky. Individual water molecules are strongly attracted to one another. Water molecules consist of two hydrogen atoms bonded to a central carbon atom. The molecule is bent at an angle of $105°$. This bent shape (as opposed to linear, $180°$) is essential to the unique properties of water. In fact, if water were a linear molecule, there would not be life anywhere in the universe. More will be said on this later. The reason water is "sticky" is that the hydrogen-oxygen bond is highly polarized. In other words, the electrons which are shared between the hydrogen and the oxygen atom in the water molecule are not shared equally. Oxygen atoms attract electrons strongly, compared to hydrogen, lending a partial negative charge to the oxygen atom and a partial positive charge to the hydrogen atom in the water molecule. See the picture below for an illustration of the polarized structure of water.

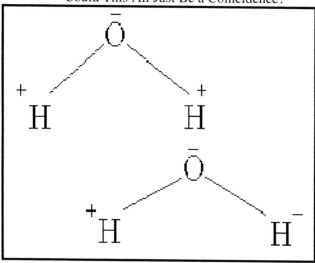

Figure 10.1 The structure of water molecules and why they are "sticky".

Another factor in water's stickiness is its shape. If water had a linear structure, rather than bent, its symmetry would make it non-polarized, despite the oxygen-hydrogen bonds in the molecule. As an example of this principle, the molecule carbon dioxide, although it has fairly polarized carbon oxygen atoms, is linear and symmetric, and therefore not polar. This non-polar molecule is therefore not sticky. Even though carbon dioxide molecules have more than twice the mass of water molecules, CO_2 becomes a gas at over one hundred degrees below zero Fahrenheit. Carbon dioxide is definitely not a molecule which could act as a solvent to support life.

When water molecules approach one another, the positively charged hydrogen atom on one molecule sticks to the negatively charged oxygen atom on the other. Due to factors beyond the discussion here, the O-H bond in molecules is the most effective of all chemical bonds at creating this stickiness. The reader may be saying to themselves 'so what' at this point. This unique stickiness of water is what results in its amazing properties as a life supporting solvent.

For example, because water molecules are so sticky, water has a very high boiling point for such a small molecule. If it

were not for the stickiness of the molecules, water would boil at
something like –200°F, way too low to support life. Besides, the
stickiness of water allows it to be a liquid over an unusually
large temperature range, an important factor in water's ability to
control climate.

Because water is so polar or sticky, it has another unique
property. Water's polarity allows it to dissolve many minerals.
There is no other molecular compound besides water which is
both liquid at the proper temperature range and able to dissolve
the ions such as sodium, calcium, chloride, magnesium,
potassium, iron and so forth which are essential to life. Water is
unique in that it can dissolve both a great variety of molecular
compounds and many ions. Chemists know water as the
"universal solvent."

The stickiness of water has an interesting effect on its solid
phase (commonly known as ice) as well. Because of the strong
intermolecular attraction between water molecules, the structure
of ice is unusually loosely packed, with a lot of space between
the atoms. For this reason, water is one of only a very small
fraction of all substances which has the property that its solid
floats in its liquid. For virtually all substances, the solid sinks in
the liquid. Why is this important? If ice did not float on water,
there would be an negative extreme effect on the environment
of the earth. In cold weather, the ice, which floats on the liquid
water, provides an insulation to the unfrozen water below. If ice
sank, whenever sufficiently cold weather struck, lakes would
freeze right to the bottom, killing most life. This in itself would
not be so bad, perhaps, but one function of water is to act as
buffer to limit the swings of global temperature. If ice did not
float on water, the temperature of the earth would swing wildly,
allowing for the possibility that during ice ages, the entire earth
could become frozen, killing off all advanced forms of life.

Water is truly a great temperature buffer. Because it is so
sticky, water is unique in that it takes a large amount of heat to
change its temperature. It takes an especially large amount of

heat to vaporize or freeze water. Most people are aware that the weather is much milder near the ocean than farther inland. This is because good old sticky water is a great climate/heat buffer. In fact, if there were no oceans of water to act as a giant heat buffer, there would be no complex life forms on earth at all, because the surface temperature would swing by hundreds of degrees annually.

There is no other compound in existence that comes even remotely close to having the properties needed to be the solvent suited to support life. Just as with carbon, the only element capable of supporting life, there is exactly one molecule capable of being the solvent for living things. Not two, one! And luckily for us, not zero either. But is it luck? If an extremely intelligent being were trying to design the properties of matter just exactly right to allow for life to exist, surely it would be forced to design a special molecule with properties just like those of water. Good job, God! Imagine the power and the intelligence of the being able not only to make something out of nothing, but also to imbue the created matter with the correct properties to form water; the solvent for life.

DESIGN AND THE BIG BANG

Startling evidence for design is found when one looks at the big bang model, as well. The outline of the big bang theory has already been described. In this section it will be shown that some of the details of the physics of the big bang reveal that the initial creation of the universe was fine-tuned to allow for life. To quote from Nobel Prize-winning physicist Steven Weinberg,[1] "Life as we know it would be impossible if any of several physical quantities had slightly different values." Weinberg goes on to relate that "One constant does seem to require incredible fine tuning." These are the words of an avowed non-believer in creation.

---

[1] Steven Weinberg, "Life in the Universe", *Scientific American*, October, 1994.

Weinberg is referring to the total energy of the Big Bang. According to the theoretical models for the big bang, if the total energy of the universe, created at the big bang, had been either bigger or smaller than it was by just one part in 1×10^{120}, life would never have formed. That is if the total amount of energy in the big bang had been different by one part in a thousand, billion, billion, billion, billion, billion, billion, billion, billion, billion, billion, billion, billion, billion, then no life would have ever formed. This is not just the word of one noted physicist. The most respected cosmologist of our generation, Stephen Hawking has described in detail this amazing coincidence which allowed the universe to produce galaxies, stars, planets, and eventually life. Another noted astrophysicist from the University of Chicago, Michael Turner, has used an analogy to describe the amazing accuracy of how well tuned the universe is to producing life. "The precision" of the creation of energy in the big bang "is as if one could throw a dart across the entire universe and hit a bulls-eye one millimeter in diameter on the other side." As Hawking has described, if there was even infinitesimally more energy in the big bang, matter would have never condensed in a way which eventually allowed for the formation of galaxies, stars and so forth. On the other hand, if the energy of the big bang had been infinitesimally smaller than it was, the entire universe would have crashed in on itself in a relatively very short time, never expanding out to a sufficient size to allow for the formation of galaxies, stars, planets, and, of course, life.

This coincidence is so astounding that those who choose to hold to an atheistic, naturalistic view have been forced to make an incredible proposal. Recently, physicists have proposed that there are an unlimited number of parallel universes. According to this model, each universe has slightly different laws. It is just a huge coincidence that the universe we happen to live in was formed with just the right properties to allow for life. Do these people have any direct evidence of these parallel universes? Of course not. Why, then, do they propose these parallel universes?

Because the thought that our universe was carefully and intelligently designed is repugnant to them. It is outside the range of possibilities they are willing to consider. For many scientists, making the atheistic assumption, the anthropic principle is rejected on philosophic principle.

The amount of energy in the universe is not the only evidence from the basic laws of physics for design. As quoted above, Steven Weinberg mentions that there are "several physical quantities" which had to have a very specific value to allow for a universe which includes life. These coincidental values are no secret to physicists. They are the motivation for some to believe in the anthropic principle, as mentioned above.

Among the physical quantities which are just right to support life, one could include the strong nuclear force which holds nuclei together. If it had been just slightly weaker, atoms larger than hydrogen would never have formed, and there would be no life. If it had been just very slightly larger, only larger atoms would have formed, and there would have been no hydrogen, no stars, no fusion in stars, and therefore no life. Apparently, God calculated in his "head" the size of strong nuclear force required, and just set it at the proper value. Good going, God! Can any human even imagine having the ability to set the strong nuclear force to be just right?

Other cosmic coincidences (which are, of course, not coincidences at all, but further evidence for design) include the size of the electromagnetic force, which holds the electrons on atoms. If it had been just a little different, then carbon and water would not have the required properties as described above. One could also mention the size of the gravitational force (responsible for the formation of galaxies, stars and planets), the amount of mass in the universe, and the initial temperature of the big bang.[2] All of these values are just in the correct range to

---

[2] A more detailed discussion can be found in Gerald L. Schroeder, *The Science of God*,
(Broadway Books, New York, 1997).

allow for life. How was the size of the gravity force set? Physicists themselves are unable to explain why gravity is as strong as it is. The anthropic principle, the idea that the universe was created with just the right natural laws to support life can explain it. In the article mentioned above, Weinberg lists a number of other cosmic coincidences. These include the extremely slight difference between the amount of matter and antimatter in the original creation. The tiny asymmetry in the amount of matter and antimatter—one part in ten trillion—allowed for matter, and eventually life to form.

The more one looks at scientific knowledge, the more one finds evidence that virtually every aspect of how the universe, the solar system, the earth and life were formed shows the work of a careful, intelligent, powerful creator behind it all. Indeed, this chapter could stretch on with example after example of design in nature. They are the fingerprints of God. The reader is left with the job of going out there and looking for the marks of God in nature for themselves. They will not have far to look.

FOR TODAY

1. Can you explain to yourself why the author does not accept the migration of the arctic   tern as convincing proof of design (despite the fact that arctic terns are clearly designed)?

2. Can you think of any aspects of nature which, to you, show the fingerprint of God?

APPENDIX

A Closer Look at the Laws of Thermodynamics

In chapter four of this book, the application of the laws of thermodynamics to the question of the origin of life was introduced. There are some more subtle and technical questions which could arise concerning the use of thermodynamics to investigate whether life could have originated spontaneously. For a person already anticipating these questions, this appendix is necessary. It is hoped that for those with less science background who are willing to wade through some admittedly more technical discussion this appendix will prove helpful as well.

This material has been relegated to an appendix, rather than the body of chapter four, because the subject is abstract enough that it could actually get in the way of what is hopefully a simple but compelling argument for most readers.

The arguments in chapter four can stand on their own. However for those with some scientific background legitimate questions can and have come up which deserve a more thorough treatment. The author has been asked the questions raised here a number of times in a variety of settings. This appendix is an effort to answer some of these questions.

The question of the relationship between the creation of life and the laws of nature deserves a closer look. Could life have been created by a "natural process"? In order to take this closer look, the laws of thermodynamics will be discussed more thoroughly to see how they apply to the specific claims of the atheists for a natural explanation of the origins of life.

The first law of thermodynamics, simply stated, is as follows: "In any process, the total energy of the universe is conserved." In other words, for any natural process, energy may change forms or move from one place to another, but the total energy in the universe is constant. No one scientist is given credit for discovering this law. However, the brewer and physicist James Prescott Joule, after whom the metric unit of energy is named, played perhaps the single greatest role in developing this concept. In the early 1800s, Joule performed experiments showing the relationship between mechanical energy and heat. By the middle of the nineteenth century, this law was considered to be more or less proven by the scientific community.

Examples of application of the "first law" would be in energy conversions such as in burning gasoline. When gasoline is burned, chemical energy in the molecules is converted to heat and light. The amount of heat and light energy produced will exactly equal the amount of chemical energy used up. If the heat produced is harnessed in an internal combustion engine, the chemical energy will be turned into heat (lost out the muffler and the radiator as well as due to friction with the road and the air), into mechanical energy to move the car, and into electrical energy to run the lights, the stereo and so forth. In any case, the total amount of energy produced will exactly equal the total energy consumed. This law has been extensively confirmed in many independent experiments, to the point that scientists take it as a given fact in approaching any problem they are faced with.

Another conservation law was discovered at about the same time as the law of conservation of energy. This law, called the law of conservation of mass, was established through some very elegant experiments done by the chemist Antoine Lavoissier in the late 18th century. The law can be simply stated as follows: "In any natural process, the total mass of the universe is conserved." In other words, in any process which can occur matter is neither created nor destroyed.

In the year 1905, Albert Einstein threw a wrench into this neat conservation law with his theory of special relativity. As part of this theory he proposed that matter can be converted into energy and energy into matter. This fact is expressed in the famous equation $E = mc^2$. This law states that the amount of energy created (or used up) in a process is equal to the amount of mass used up (or created) in the process times the square of the speed of light. Examples of applications of this law are nuclear fusion or fission, in which atoms are built up or split apart releasing huge amounts of energy. In normal chemical reactions, the amount of energy involved (E) is so small the amount of mass change (m) is too small to be measured by any standard mass-measuring device, which explains why the law of conservation of mass was accepted for so long. A combined law may be expressed in a more general first law of thermodynamics as follows: "In any process, the total of mass and energy of the universe are conserved."

The first law of thermodynamics amounts to a mathematics of natural processes. It does not predict whether a particular process can happen; only the result in terms of energy if it does. This law is extremely limited in its ability to help one decide whether life was created. As an example of this fact, consider a rock balanced on the edge of a cliff. If it were to leave the edge of the cliff, it is easy to predict what would happen—it would fall! Knowledge of the laws of thermodynamics is not needed to predict this. However, one can apply the first Law to this event by describing what happens in terms of energy. When the rock falls, gravitational potential energy is turned into kinetic energy as the rock accelerates. Some of the energy is lost as heat due to friction with the air. What happens to the kinetic energy when the rock hits the ground? The answer is that it is turned into heat (as well as a little bit of sound energy). If a person quickly went and felt the ground where the rock hit, they would notice it got just a little bit warmer.

Here is where the limitations of the first law of thermodynamics become clear. There is nothing in the first law which precludes all the heat energy in the ground coming together and spontaneously causing the rock to be thrown off the ground, up into the air, and back up onto the cliff. One knows intuitively that this process is impossible, but the first law of thermodynamics cannot explain why. If a film was seen showing a large rock suddenly rising off the ground into the air and landing in a delicately balanced position on top of a cliff, the viewer would be absolutely convinced the film was being run backward. The conclusion is that some processes in nature are only spontaneous in one direction and not the reverse. Well, not quite! If a person used intelligence and planning, they could pick up the boulder and carry it up to the top of the cliff, replacing it in its original position on top of the cliff. This apparent exception to the law of spontaneity will be revisited later.

The example above reveals the fact that certain things simply never could happen. Occasionally, when a large, old building is beyond the point of being renovated, it is demolished using carefully placed explosives. Most people have seen a recording of a large building being taken down, producing a huge cloud of dust and a large pile of rubble. It is obvious that the pile of rubble and cloud of dust could never spontaneously join themselves together to reform a building with all the pipes soldered together and all the bricks laid straight, cemented in position, etc. This would be absolutely impossible. There is a myriad of similar examples of the principle of processes being irreversible. It is interesting to note that although a building could never spontaneously simply come together, buildings do exist. They require an intelligent creator, willing to plan carefully and work hard in order to bring the different components into a carefully ordered state.

The principle by which scientists explain what processes can occur spontaneously and which cannot is the second law of thermodynamics. Nothing in the first law precludes the possibility of the blown up building being recreated spontaneously out of its dust and rubble. However, the "second law" of thermodynamics can be used to predict that this process in not possible.

Unfortunately, the second law of thermodynamics is more abstract than the first. It is difficult to state in a way easily understood by the uninitiated. One of the earliest statements of the second law is as follows. "Heat flows spontaneously from hot to cold objects, but not from cold objects to hot objects." In other words, if you put a hot rock into cold water, the rock would cool off, while the water would get hotter. It is impossible for the hot rock to suck even more heat out of the cooler water, causing the cold water to get even colder. It is tempting to say in response, "I did not need some scientist to tell me that one." This is true. However, using this law in the carefully stated form of an equation, the French physicist Sadi Carnot was able to predict that it is impossible to create a perpetual motion machine— one whose sole function is to convert heat into mechanical energy with 100% efficiency. The work of Carnot and others to improve the efficiency of steam engines by applying the second law of thermodynamics to the problem contributed greatly to the industrial revolution in the nineteenth century.

A later formulation of the second law is that of Claussius. This statement is of relevance to chemistry, and therefore to the question of the origins of life. It could be stated as follows: "For any spontaneous process, the entropy of the universe increases." Loosely stated, entropy is a measure of randomness or freedom of motion. The reader may not want to know the actual definition of entropy as a physicist would state it, but here it is anyway. "The entropy of a process is the heat of that process, done in a reversible way, divided by the absolute temperature of the process." If the temperature is not constant while a process occurs, calculus must be used to define entropy.

In any case, one now has a rule to predict whether any process will occur spontaneously. A process which creates more "order" in the universe will not be spontaneous. Consider a few processes which increase entropy. In doing so, one will see that the concept of entropy is perhaps a bit more intuitive than expected. For example, if ice, in which the water molecules are locked into a definite position, is melted, the molecules are allowed to move about with random motion in the liquid. This increased freedom of motion implies that the entropy of water is greater than that of ice. Similarly, when water is boiled, entropy is increased because the water molecules are no longer attached to one another in steam as they were in water, allowing for more freedom of motion.

Clearly, blowing up a building dramatically increases entropy. On the other hand, the creation of a large building with so much "order," with all the bricks lined up just right and all the wires attached at the right places requires a very large decrease in entropy. It therefore will not happen spontaneously.

What about chemistry? Large molecules such as DNA, proteins, complex lipids and sugars are in a very low state of entropy. Creating these macromolecules from smaller ones (a necessary process in order for life to be created spontaneously) involves a large decrease of entropy. This is true, not only because of the size of the molecules—involving in some cases hundreds of thousands of atoms—but also because of the great degree of order in the structure, for example, of proteins. In order for an enzyme to function, not only do many different amino acid molecules need to come together spontaneously, the correct number of each of the twenty naturally occurring amino acids have to be joined in exactly the right order for the enzyme to work. If the primordial soup from which life is supposed to have been created contained any besides the twenty correct amino acids (and it unquestionably would), they would have to be excluded from the structure. Not only this, but the enzyme molecule must be arranged geometrically in exactly the right shape to function.

Even if by chance a large, complex, ordered thing such as a DNA molecule or an enzyme were somehow to come to exist, the second law could be used to predict that the molecule, if subject to the vagaries of the environment, would soon fall apart. It would decompose to smaller, more random chunks of molecule, with more entropy. This is why, as mentioned earlier, Nobel prize-winning chemist Melvin Calvin said that when looking at very old sediments under bogs, they do not even look for proteins or polysaccharides (sugars), because it is a matter of common knowledge that these molecules are not stable.[1] Why atheists theorize that these molecules slowly built up and evolved into more and more complex structures in some ancient earth environment seems to be beyond explanation. It is also beyond the second law of thermodynamics.

Perhaps at this point the reader would say, "Well, there you go. It is proven. Obviously life was created." However, it is not quite that simple. Processes which decrease entropy do in some cases occur. For example, water can be frozen! Under the right conditions, ice can be created out of water, even though this results in a decrease in entropy. What about this? More importantly, living things clearly do exist and they have very low entropy. Aren't they violations of the second law of thermodynamics? In order to approach these questions, an even closer look is required.

The ice-from-water example will provide a good illustration. It turns out that the statement of the second law of thermodynamics given above, although correct, needs to be put more carefully to be useful. This is true, because entropy can decrease in one place, as long as it increases somewhere else at the same time by an even greater amount. For example, when water freezes the entropy of the water decreases. However, when the heat leaves the water to go into the environment (for example in your freezer), it increases the entropy of the environment even more than it decreases the entropy of the water. Consider a situation in which as some water freezes, the

---

[1] Melvin Calvin, *Chemical Evolution* (Oregon State System of Higher Education, Eugene, Oregon, 1961), p. 34.

change of entropy in the water is S = -10 entropy units. S is the conventional symbol for entropy. If the environment increases in entropy because of the heat it absorbs from the water by S = +15 entropy units, then the total entropy change for the process is S = -10 + 15 = +5 entropy units. In this case the total change of entropy of the universe is positive, and the water will freeze spontaneously.

It just so happens that below zero degrees centigrade (32 degrees Fahrenheit) the total entropy change for water to turn to ice is positive, and water freezes spontaneously. Above zero degrees centigrade the entropy change for water to freeze becomes negative and water will not freeze. Therefore a scientist could predict the freezing point of water to be zero degrees centigrade using the second law of thermodynamics!

Evidently, the simple fact that a process has a negative entropy change is not a sufficient predictor of whether or not it will be spontaneous. In order to make this concept useful for one trying to predict whether a process will be spontaneous, one could create four possible scenarios, described in the table below.

Scenario	S system	S surroundings
#1	positive	positive
#2	positive	negative
#3	negative	positive
#4	negative	negative

A process described by the first scenario would definitely have total entropy change which is positive, so it would definitely be spontaneous. A process described by the fourth scenario would definitely have a negative total entropy change and it would therefore definitely not occur spontaneously. Whether a process described by case #2 or #3 would be spontaneous would depend on the temperature. For example, water freezing to form ice would fit into scenario #3, so it can occur, but only at sufficiently low temperatures. An example of scenario #1 would be paper burning to form carbon dioxide and water. This is a spontaneous process. An example of scenario #4 would be for carbon dioxide and water to come together to form paper. This would require absorption of heat from the environment, making the entropy change of the environment negative. It would also require the formation of very complex cellulose molecules making the entropy change of the system negative. The conclusion is that paper will not form spontaneously under any circumstances no matter how much heat one puts into a mixture of the proper gases. No matter how long one waits, it will never happen!

The same criterion could be applied to the supposed processes by which Carl Sagan, Melvin Calvin and other atheists claim life came to be by a spontaneous process. The processes by which the basic molecules of life (carbohydrates, lipids, proteins and nucleic acids) are created from simpler building blocks all absorb heat from the environment; therefore they have a negative entropy change in the environment. They all result in a decrease in entropy in the molecules as well. This is scenario #4 described above. Because it is an example of case #4, it can be predicted that paper spontaneously appearing out of a jar of carbon dioxide and water is impossible. Similarly one can conclude that molecules such as enzymes would never appear spontaneously out of a soup of simple molecules even if one waited indefinitely. And this is just considering the spontaneous production of one functioning enzyme molecule. It is a great leap from this point to even begin to consider the production (simultaneously and at the same place) of thousands of different molecules of lipids, carbohydrates, proteins and nucleic acids—all coming together to form a unit which is able to ingest food, grow, and reproduce.

But there is still one more question to be answered. This is probably the hardest one to deal with of all. Clearly paper exists. Clearly living things exist. Even if God created living things, does not the very continued existence of living things constitute a violation of the second law of thermodynamics? Don't living things have to make proteins, nucleic acids and so forth, in apparent violation of the second law? It is time to answer this intriguing question.

How can life exist with its extreme amount of order; with its unaccountably low entropy? The answer is that all living things have an energy-fixing mechanism. In other words, all living things have the ability to derive usable energy from their environment, and to use that energy to decrease entropy (to synthesize large, ordered molecules). A living thing has an extremely complex set of metabolic pathways; a series of chemical steps controlled by enzyme molecules which it uses to turn food into the raw materials (sugars, fats or amino acids) for metabolism, eventually converting the energy in food into such energy-storing molecules as ATP (adenosine triphosphate). The energy stored in these molecules allows the living cell to synthesize large protein and nucleic acid molecules—those molecules which allow a living thing to eat, grow, reproduce, think etc.

The bottom line is that if energy is used in a carefully controlled way, it can be used to reduce entropy locally at the expense of increasing entropy globally. A simple example of this is in a refrigerator. A refrigerator moves heat from a cold place to a hot place. At first glance this would be in direct violation of the original statement of the second law above. However, it happens that the second law allows for the possibility of energy being used to decrease entropy locally, if it is incorporated into a system in a carefully controlled way. The point to be made here is that a refrigerator would never just happen. It takes a thinking, planning designer to create a device such as a refrigerator. The same is true, except to an inconceivably greater degree, in the design of a living thing.

One of my favorite subjects to teach is biochemistry. In studying this subject one gets a glance at the overwhelming chemical complexity of even the simplest living system. This sort of thing, with its great order (and very low entropy), is made possible because a very intelligent designer created a chemical system which can incorporate food energy in such a way which allows the system to synthesize the very chemicals which allowed it to incorporate the food in the first place. Which came first, the chicken or the egg?

This brings the argument to the last stand of the atheist in defending their natural explanation of the origins of life. They would claim that if sufficient energy were available (presumably from sunlight, although other energy sources are possible), given the right building blocks, and sufficient time, entropy could be reduced enough in some local environment to spontaneously produce a living thing. Given our description of how a refrigerator works, this almost sounds plausible.

In fact, if sufficient energy is input to a system in a non-intelligent way, thermal entropy may be reduced, but informational entropy cannot. The distinction between the two types of entropy may be defined by analogy. Consider an explosion such as the one which occurs in an internal combustion engine. This explosive energy can be used to compress a gas (decreasing the thermal entropy), which ultimately moves a piston in the engine, causing a car to move up a hill (a process normally not spontaneous because it decreases the gross amount of entropy). Another example of energy being used to decrease thermal entropy is in a refrigerator. Here either electrical or chemical energy is used up to carry heat from a cold to a warm place, decreasing entropy.

None of these examples involve a decrease in *informational* entropy. Consider a room with a bunch of playing cards randomly distributed on the floor. Now, consider a backward vacuum cleaner pointed at the cards as a source of energy. It could be used to push all the cards into the corner, decreasing the "thermal entropy." However, it could not be used to separate the cards into neatly piled suits or to build a house of cards. Energy could only be used to build a house of cards if the energy were directed by design. Simply throwing energy at a system will never decrease the informational entropy of that system to a significant degree.

Figure 9.1 Illustration: An example of energy creating disorder, not order. An earthquake caused a building to collapse in the Marina District, San Francisco, CA.

The refrigerator provides a further example. A refrigerator can be used to reduce entropy, using up electrical energy to reduce thermal entropy. However throwing a bunch of energy at the raw materials needed to produce a refrigerator could never result in the production of a refrigerator. There is no way that one could take a pile of iron ore and crude petroleum (as well as all the other raw materials required to build a refrigerator), and then simply add energy and wait long enough for a refrigerator to result, with the nuts screwed into the holes, the belt on the motor and so forth. Rather, a designer is required to direct the flow of energy needed to create the refrigerator. There is no way around this. G. Nicolas and Nobel Prize winning I. Prigogine have discussed the distinction between reducing thermal and informational entropy as it relates to the origin of life.

> Needless to say, these simple remarks cannot suffice to solve the problem of prebiological order. One would like not only to establish that the Second Law (S>0) is compatible with a decrease in the overall (system) entropy (S<0), but also to indicate the mechanisms responsible for the emergence and maintenance of coherent states. [2]

Prigogine and Nicolis point out here that it is not enough to show that overall system entropy (what I am calling thermal entropy) can be reduced by inputting energy. The question to be asked is how did "prebiological order" or "coherent states" come to be? Scientists have no answer to this question, or they refer to "chemical evolution" and "sufficient time" as the explanations. Use of these nice-sounding terms does nothing to change the fact that more and more energy and more and more time will always yield disorder and an increase in informational entropy. Information simply does not gradually increase in nature without an intelligent injection of energy.

Many examples of informational entropy being reduced could be given, but all require an initial design. Consider a blank cassette tape. It contains magnetic material which, when the tape is bought, is randomly oriented (high entropy). When an electric signal proportional to the sound of a musical instrument is run through the record head, the magnetic field on the tape is unrandomized (low entropy), producing sufficient order that it is able to cause music to be played back when the magnetic signal is read. Does anyone believe that the same tape could be randomly magnetized or demagnetized by some mechanism, and suddenly at a later time by some amazing accident a piece of music could just spontaneously just appear on the tape? No! This would require a large reduction in informational entropy. It could only be done by intelligent design.

---

[2] G. Nicolis and I. Prigogine, *Self-Organization in Non-equilibrium Systems*, Wiley, 1977, p. 23.

Even the simplest living organism is much more complex and has inconceivably more order than a house of cards or the cassette tape of a musical piece. In other words, the probability of a backward vacuum cleaner being applied to a pile of playing cards producing a well-designed house of cards is much greater than the chances of a prebiological soup producing even one usable gene, never mind all the thousands of proteins, carbohydrates, nucleic acids and lipids needed to produce a living thing.

In fact, the probability of a house of cards being built by a backward vacuum cleaner is not just small, it is zero. Even if by some amazing coincidence all the cards would just happen to be in the right position to be a house at some instant in time, the very vacuum which created the house in the first place would instantaneously destroy it. This is another example of the illogical idea of proposing unlimited energy to create a large degree of order. The large amount of energy required to decrease the entropy in a chemical system (or a group of cards) would very quickly randomize that information, even if it were momentarily produced.

Remember that "sufficient time" does not change this argument in the slightest. Very unlikely events will have their probability increased by waiting. However, impossible events, which grossly decrease informational entropy without the intervention of a creator will not become more possible with time. As an example, the probability of a very large asteroid hitting the earth this year is extremely low. However, it can be predicted that in the time span of a billion years, this very small probability would accumulate to the point that the event actually becomes quite likely over that very great time span. Consider the reverse process, the impossible one. Imagine running an asteroid collision backward. In other words, imagine billions of dust particles, small rocks, many huge boulders as well as a great deal of gases spontaneously joining themselves together to become a giant asteroid, which then lifts itself off the surface of the earth to be hurtled back into space. This is an impossible event, whose probability will not grow with time. The exact concept applies to the formation of life without a creator.

Again, a number of examples and analogies could be quoted, but hopefully the point is made. It is tempting to quote statistics and probabilities, such as the probability of making a particular chain of protein out of a random sample of amino acids, or the probability of excluding other extraneous molecules at the same time and so forth.

Throwing out extremely small numbers and multiplying them to produce even smaller numbers could go on ad infinitum. In the end, the probability of even a single usable molecule of DNA being produced is zero. The interested reader will find an excellent reference which covers both the probability arguments and the informational entropy concept more thoroughly.[3]

In summary, the laws of thermodynamics imply that life could never have just happened by a natural process. No amount of scientific fast talk will change this fact. The reason many scientists cling to the natural explanation for the origin of life is either a lack of sufficient understanding of the relevant scientific laws, or more likely, an unwillingness to throw away their pre-conceived assumption that the natural laws can explain everything that ever has or ever will happen.

---

[3] Walter L. Bradley, "Thermodynamics of the Origins of Life," *Journal of the American Scientific Affiliation*, June 1988.

Order Form
Great Commission Illustrated Books
Order On-line at http://greatcommission.com

Name_____Address_____

City_____State_____ Zip_____

Phone_____Nation_____

Email Address_____

If the order includes ten or more of an individual item, a discount of
25% applies to that item's Line Total. If you include proof of
purchase of previous version of *The Explorers of Ararat,* take 25%
off retail price below.

Item	Quantity	Price	Total
Is There A God? Science & Bible		$10.95	
Explorers of Ararat: Noah's Ark Search		$24.95	
Keeping the Faith: Early Church		$14.95	
Born of Water: The Bible on Baptism		$ 8.95	
Grass Really Isn't Greener: Restoration		$ 8.95	
In the Beginning: Evolution, Flood		$17.95	
		Sub-Total	
	Postage & Handling		
CA residents add 7.25% Sales Tax			
		Total	

For U.S. orders, please include $4.00 postage and handling for the
first item ordered, and 50 cents for each additional item. For other
countries, add $10.00 for the first item plus $5.00 for each additional
item. Orders outside USA, send money order payable in U.S. dollars
on U.S. banks only.

Great Commission Illustrated Books (GCI)
4208 Stanbridge Ave.
Long Beach CA 90808-1649
http://greatcommission.com
books@greatcommission.com